D1827036

Developing English with young learners

by Opal Dunn

Essential Language Teaching Series

General Editor: Roger H Flavell

MODERN ENGLISH PUBLICATIONS

First published 1984
Reprinted 1989 (twice), 1990, 1991, 1992 (twice), 1993

Published by MACMILLAN PUBLISHERS LTD
London and Basingstoke

ISBN 0 – 333 – 35335 – 8

Printed in China

The author and publishers are grateful to
Modern English Publications Ltd for
permission to reproduce an illustration from
Teaching English, ed. Susan Holden, 1980.

The author and publishers wish to
acknowledge with thanks, the following
photographic sources: The Greater London
Council and Jean-Jacques Dunn.

Contents

About this book

This book is the result of many years of teaching and training teachers of young children in the Far East, Europe and North Africa. It is written for teachers of young children. In this context young children cannot be thought of only in chronological terms; personal development and cultural background play an important role in the readiness of a child to learn. Whereas in *Beginning English with young children* (Dunn 1983) the emphasis is on a child's early years, this book moves on to consider the beginnings of reading and writing.

In this book, the terms EFL, ESL and bilingual are used to describe the learning situations found in schools and classrooms throughout the world (for an explanation of these terms see Dunn 1983: 19). Language 1 is taken to refer to the mother tongue, or the language used in school if it is other than the mother tongue. For convenience, English is mostly referred to as Language 2 (L2). The child is referred to as 'he' and the teacher as 'she', as most of the teachers the author has met are women.

Examples that make abstract ideas concrete are taken from the author's experience. These, together with charts, checklists and other illustrative material, should make the book helpful to teachers in EFL, ESL or bilingual teaching situations.

Many people believe that children in EFL, ESL or bilingual learning situations all pass through approximately the same beginning stages, acquiring language in more or less the same order. For convenience, the author refers to these stages as Part One of a syllabus. By the end of Part One, children can use a little language well and are ready, in Part Two, to cope with the wider syllabus and more varied and less predictable activities of a language-learning programme. Chapter 5 focuses on Part Two of a beginner's syllabus.

The language young beginners learn to read and write must already be within their oral vocabulary. For this reason, *Beginning English with young children* deals with oral acquisition, and this book develops reading, handwriting and writing skills. *Developing English with young learners* considers the teaching of these skills, and of written communication. Suggestions are given for reading and handwriting programmes and lesson planning. There are ideas and instructions for many activities and games which involve reading and writing. Chapter 5 considers in more detail the difference between Part One and Part Two of a syllabus and looks ahead to the teaching of post-beginners.

Local situations differ from country to country and classroom to classroom, and each child is an individual requiring individual attention. For this reason, there can obviously be no one teaching method and no one text suitable for all children. What is written in this book is based on experience and study and an effort to see things not only from the teacher's point of view, but also from that of the child. The intention and hope is that it should be flexible enough to be used in the wide variety of situations throughout the world in which English is taught to young beginners.

1 Beginning reading

Reading is a complex process and it is astonishing how children manage to do it so well at such a young age. It involves 'decoding' or working out the meaning of unknown words on the page and, in the light of their past experience, making sense of the whole. Children's ability to read in a foreign language is even more remarkable, but is often underestimated and sometimes under-utilised.

1.1 Introducing reading

Many foreigners are surprised that learning to read in English for some native English speakers is not easy and in some cases takes several years. They are amazed that there is no one set method or set textbook used by every school for teaching reading. In England when children go to school, they are exposed to a 'learning-to-read programme' which may follow a blend of reading methods, using specially written books which are lexically graded, from one or more reading schemes. Children work at their own speed and some complete a reading scheme in one or two terms, others in two years.

Children who have learned what reading is about can read a certain number of words by sight (see Figure 1). Once they have seen a word five, twenty or perhaps thirty times (the number depends on their maturity and ability) they can recognise it and read it by themselves without having to decode it or to be told how to read it. This is called sight recognition.

Figure 1 Methods of teaching reading to native English speakers

	Method	**Technique**
Based on information about letters which make up words	Alphabetic	Teaches names of letters
	New phonic	Teaches a linguistic analysis blending sounds of letters to make words Texts based on words not structures
Based on recognition of meaningful words, phrases or sentences without knowledge of sounds of letters	Whole word or Look and say	Teaches sight recognition of whole words often selected from child's own experience
	Whole sentences	Teaches sight recognition of phrases and sentences Encourages reading for meaning with stress and intonation
Based on recognition of children's spoken language – words, phrases, sentences	Language experience approach (children's language method)	Teaches texts based on children's own language

Comment	Example
Gives insufficient information for some children to work out their own method of decoding Confusion can arise between letters nearly the same shape or sound, eg *b d g*	cat *c* – /si/ *a* – /ei/ *t* – /ti/
Initial progress slow and sometimes discouraging and confusing for very young children Many common words are exceptions to rules To give practice it is sometimes necessary to use words not useful to children Children need good auditory ability to hear different sounds	cat *c* – /k/ *a* – /æ/ *t* – /t/ Meg, the peg-leg, has a pet hen (Morris et al. 1974)
Initial progress is fast giving child confidence to face later problems Can lead to guessing or dependency on adult for introduction of new words Children have to work out their own method of decoding which may be difficult for children who have not been introduced to sounds of letters There can be confusion between words looking the same, eg *doing, going* Service words, eg *the, in, up, on* are sometimes omitted in reading	elephant dog book television The book is on the table John's birthday party (see Murray 1969)
Gives opportunity: 1　to introduce naturally the relationship between letter and sound 2　to expand vocabulary 3　to explain differences between spoken and written language	This is the fire engine I saw (see Mackay et al. 1970)

To decode words children use clues often unconsciously from several methods, combining them in the most economical way to get information. Some of the clues which they may use either individually or in combination are given in Figure 2.

Figure 2 Clues to reading

Shape of the word
Length
Letters above or below the line
Initial and/or final letter
Letter pattern within the word

egg elephant
dog bat
playing

Sound of the word
Based on letter/sound knowledge (phonics)
The sound of a word is worked out and possibly related to previous oral experience

Position of the word in the structure
Prediction of unrecognised word from previous use of spoken language

From context
Information obtained from the text gives clues to the unrecognised word

From the illustration
Illustration backs up text by providing the clues

In literate societies, most children learn almost unaided and from a very young age to recognise the names or logos of their favourite ice cream or sweets, the name of a brand of petrol and the names of other things which interest them. Many teachers have found it successful to begin teaching reading by building on this already existing skill and developing children's ability to recognise whole words by sight. By using this 'whole word' approach, children can quickly reach the point where they can read simple books, which is what they long to do. This early success motivates them and gives them confidence to tackle the problems they encounter on the way to becoming fluent decoders.

1.2 Reading programme

Children who have already learned to read in their mother tongue or language of instruction have understood the technical features of written language and the communicative nature of reading. They have also developed sufficient muscular co-ordination of eye and hand movements to read print. For these children, learning to read in English involves merely transferring their Language 1 reading skills and applying them, when relevant, to reading in English (see Dunn 1983: Chapter 1). Since most teachers will be working with children who can already read and write in Language 1, preparing children to develop reading skills is dealt with later in this chapter.

Children whose Language 1 is written in Roman script, for example French, Dutch or Malay, learn to read in English amazingly quickly, if motivated. If they have an oral knowledge of the language used in early books, they quickly pass through the stage of reading word by word to reading in phrases, with good pronunciation, intonation and stress.

Children whose language is not coded in Roman script, for example Arabic, Japanese or Chinese, first have to be taught the Roman script (see Chapter 2). As Arabic is written from right to left, and most Japanese primary school textbooks from the top to the bottom of the page, this involves getting used to different eye movements when learning English. Although this takes a little time, children seem to take it in their stride. Young children at this age are learning new things all the time. Some may be learning another form of reading in learning to read music. Also the fact that they have already developed sufficient muscular control of their eye movements to be able to read print means that they can quickly adjust to different eye movements.

When beginning a reading programme, teachers should first introduce texts which children already know orally. This helps the children to get on quickly and to read with correct pronunciation, stress and intonation. It also avoids the situation where children whose Language 1 is written in Roman letters use Language 1 clues for decoding English, because they have not yet acquired the necessary information to be able to decode in English. This kind of mistake can be seen in the inset below.

AGE	10
GROUP SIZE	1
BACKGROUND	Language 1 = French; an EFL situation
SCHOOL	French language primary school
	Private EFL class outside school hours

The child was asked to read aloud a simple text in English. This was the first time he had seen the text; some of the words he recognised by sight, others he had not encountered orally. He read the words he had already encountered with English pronunciation; the new words he read with French pronunciation. He was, in fact, using a French sound system to decode the new words as he had not been taught phonics and had not been sufficiently exposed to written English to have worked out his own sound system for decoding English.

If the text is already known orally and children have had new words introduced by flash cards, it is not necessary for them to fall back on their Language 1 decoding methods. Once children get into the habit of using other decoding methods for reading English, it takes quite a long time to break the habit.

Some children, however, when they have acquired sight recognition of about fifty to seventy words, start developing their own personal decoding. Provided they are given plenty of language and reading experience, these children go on to become good decoders.

Other children, when they have sight recognition of about 100–150 words, need help to acquire information on sound/letter relationships. They can then use this information to decode words. If they are not helped beyond the stage of sight recognition of 'whole words', they will not be able to tackle new words by themselves. The introduction of sound/letter recognition is best based on words already within the children's experience.

At this stage, it is helpful for all learners to make a picture dictionary (see Section 1.6 of this chapter). In making the dictionary, children are introduced through words they already know orally to the initial consonants and vowels. In Part One it is confusing for children to be introduced to other phonic rules. Children will also profit from language experiences like being read to, reciting and learning rhymes, which expose children in a natural way to the complete sound system of the English language.

By the end of Part One, children should have acquired sufficient skill in reading simple texts to be able to use most of the clues to reading suggested in Figure 2. The reading programme shown in Figure 3 has been found successful with young beginners in Part One.

Figure 3   Reading programme

Step one
Introduction of small letters (lower case) of the alphabet, using the names (eg /eɪ/ for the letter *a*) not the sounds (phonemes) (eg /æ/, as the letter *a* is often pronounced)

Step two

Introduction of whole words from the first reading book by flash cards (the children already know the text orally)

Introduction of capital letters (upper case) of the alphabet, using the names not the sounds (phonemes)

Step three

Introduction of more whole words, taken from the first reading book, by flash cards

Introduction of simple reading texts: stories, workbooks, rhymes, etc

Step four

Introduction of whole words or phrases by flash cards

Reading simple texts

Introduction of some initial consonant sounds by making a picture dictionary

Step five

New words now introduced without flash cards

Reading simple texts

Further introduction of initial consonants by making a picture dictionary

Step six

Further reading experiences: notices, letters, games, etc

Introduction of initial short vowels by making a picture dictionary

The stage at which children pass from reading word by word to reading complete phrases and sentences meaningfully depends on their individual ability and maturity and the amount of oral introduction they have had to the text. The more practice children have in reading, the sooner they become able to read with fluency. Reading is learned by reading experience.

After completing Step six, children should be able to read simple texts easily, and be ready to go on to more difficult texts which involve decoding of new words as distinct from recognising whole words. Special attention should be given to any child who is not making progress in reading at this stage.

Throughout this programme, learning the techniques of reading should not dominate to such an extent that children forget that reading is for communication and enjoyment. During each lesson or just before the end of the lesson, teachers should find time to read a simple picture book or rhyme to children (see inset below). Ideally, children should also have their own copies of books apart from textbooks and have access to borrowing good story picture books.

AGE	8–9
GROUP SIZE	20
BACKGROUND	Language 1 = mixed; international community
SCHOOL	International ESL school
	Few English Language 1 pupils

At the end of each day, ten to fifteen minutes before going home, the children gathered on the floor round the teacher's chair. The teacher went over work done during the day, discussed work for the following day and then read part, or all, of a picture book. The choice of book was made alternately by the teacher and one of the groups in the class. The groups always chose a book the teacher had previously read; the teacher introduced a new story.

Once children have transferred their reading skills to English, their progress appears to be linked to their ability to read in Language 1. Children who are good readers in Language 1 seem also to be good readers in English and conversely, children who have reading difficulties in Language 1 often have similar difficulties in reading English. However, there are cases where a child's reading difficulties may be psychological and these psychological problems are not necessarily transferred to learning English. In such cases these children can often read better in English than in Language 1. Where children have not yet learned to read in Language 1, they need to pass through a 'reading readiness' programme before following the plan shown in Figure 3.

PREPARING YOUNG NON-READERS FOR READING

Everyday experiences at home and school help to prepare young readers for reading. Teachers and parents should bear in mind the following points in particular.

Young children may only be familiar with speech as a method of communication, and need help to realise that communication can also take place through print and writing. Special efforts should be made to point this out by reading notices, print on packets and print in books aloud to children. Labels, name cards, notices and letters to parents can be written by teachers in print handwriting (see Chapter 2) whilst children watch. As the teacher writes she should read each word aloud and then read the complete text several times, pointing to each word as she reads. It is important that print handwriting should resemble the print in the first reading books, as any difference in shape of letters confuses at this stage.

Young children may not realise that language is broken up into words and that one word generally has one meaning. Until this concept has been clearly grasped, children will find it difficult to read well. When reading rhymes and stories to children, teachers can hold up the book and point to the text, word by word. As children become more familiar with the rhyme, they can do this themselves, using their own copies, as the teacher reads. Care should be taken to see that children point to each word, one by one, accurately. In the early stages, children sometimes think that words with two syllables are in fact two words (eg *paint – ing*).

Young children need to be introduced to letters informally in rhymes, songs and games, and be helped to realise that letters make up words. Some children have difficulty in grasping the distinction between letters and words; 'a', after all, is a word and so is 'I', but each is also a letter. To avoid confusion at this stage, only the names of the letters and not the sounds (phonemes) should be taught.

Young children need to be helped to develop left-to-right eye movements as well as co-ordination between eye and hand movements. Children can be encouraged to point to words in stories and rhymes as the teacher reads, to make writing patterns (see Chapter 2), to draw and to paint. They should be given plenty of opportunity to make things with their hands. Even giving out cards for a game helps to develop muscular control.

Young children need the opportunity to learn that information and pleasure can be derived from books and that books are interesting.

Young children need to have experiences which help them realise the value and usefulness of reading, that is the value of written language as a way of storing information and recording ideas or feelings which would otherwise be lost, eg a shopping list or a poem.

TEACHING THE ALPHABET

The first step in a reading programme is to teach the alphabet. Children who can already read in Language 1 expect to be introduced to the alphabet in one of their first English lessons. If the children's Language 1 writing system is different from Roman script, they need to be given opportunities to see books printed in English before they begin to learn the alphabet. Children who have not yet learned to read can be introduced to the alphabet in their 'reading readiness' programme. The introduction is naturally much slower for these children.

There are two methods of teaching the alphabet; the teacher can either introduce the names of the letters, or she can teach the sounds of the letters (phonemes) first (see Figure 4). As some children come to the English lesson having learned the names of some of the letters from their families, from television, or from games or songs, it is advisable to build on to this knowledge, teaching the names of all the letters. To introduce the sounds of the letters at this stage could be confusing, especially as many parents do not know them and thus cannot help at home. Later, when children have confidence in reading simple texts, the

Figure 4   Names and sounds of the letters of the alphabet

Vowels	Letter name	Letter sound (phoneme)
a e i o u	/eɪ/ as in d*a*te *a*ge /i/ as in d*ee*d *e*vil /aɪ/ as in d*i*ne *i*tem /əʊ/ as in b*o*ne *o*ld /ju/ as in t*u*ne *u*se	/æ/ as in *a*t /e/ as in *e*nd /ɪ/ as in *i*n /ɒ/ as in *o*n /ʌ/ as in *u*p

Note
English vowel sounds are not perfectly consistent in their pronunciation. 'ape' and 'age' begin with the same sound, yet 'are', 'awe' and 'axe' are each different. There is a list of all the vowel sounds of English in Dunn 1983: 61.

Consonants	Letter name	Letter sound (phoneme)
b	/bi/ pronounced as the word *bee*	/b/ as in *b*in
c	/si/ pronounced as the word *sea*	/k/ as in *c*an
d	/di/ pronounced as the word *Dee*	/d/ as in *d*in
f	/ef/ as in *eff*ort	/f/ as in *f*in
g	/dʒi/ pronounced as *gee*	/g/ as in *g*one
h	/eɪtʃ/ pronounced as *aitch*	/h/ as in *h*it
j	/dʒeɪ/ pronounced as the word *jay*	/dʒ/ as in *j*eans
k	/keɪ/ as in o*kay*	/k/ as in *k*ing
l	/el/ as in *el*der	/l/ as in *l*it
m	/em/ as in *em*phasise	/m/ as in *m*eet
n	/en/ as in *en*d	/n/ as in *n*eat
p	/pi/ pronounced as the word *pea*	/p/ as in *p*in
q	/kju/ pronounced as the word *queue*	/kw/ as in *qu*een
r	/ɑ/ pronounced as the word *are*	/r/ as in *r*un
s	/es/ pronounced as in e*s*tate	/s/ as in *s*un
t	/ti/ pronounced as the word *tea*	/t/ as in *t*in
v	/vi/ as in *v*eal	/v/ as in *v*ote
w	double /ju/	/w/ as in *w*in
x	/eks/ as in e*x*tra	/ks/ as in a*x*e
y	/wɑɪ/ pronounced as the word *why*	/j/ as in *y*es
z	/zed/ to rhyme with bed	/z/ as in *z*ebra

Note
The above consonant sounds are not all those that English possesses. There is full information in another book in this series *Pronunciation skills* (Tench 1981: 7).

sounds of the letters can be introduced, based on words in the children's oral vocabulary. The alphabet song below can be used to help in consolidating the letters of the alphabet. It is a good idea to back up the song by using flash cards for the letters. Alphabet books can also provide an enjoyable reading experience, and the selection of words is useful (see *The Alphabet Book* part of *Language in Action*, Morris 1974).

The small letters of the alphabet are introduced first as these are the letters most frequently used. Depending on the age of the children and their previous reading experience, two, three or four letters can be introduced in each lesson. Four different flash cards for each letter are suggested as this gives four complete learning experiences.

Step one

a Hold up a flash card of small *a* and say 'a' 'a' 'a' (phonetically this is /eɪ/ not /æ/).

b Repeat as above with a second flash card of small *a*.

c Hold up a third flash card and children say with the teacher 'a' 'a' 'a'.

d Repeat with a fourth flash card.

> **Step two**
> a Revise the flash cards.
> b Introduce new flash cards as in Step One.
> c Play the *Flash Card Game* (see Section 3).

Once children can recognise the twenty-six lower case letters of the alphabet, they are ready to begin writing (see Chapter 2). They should not be introduced to capital (upper case) letters until they have consolidated the use of lower case letters. The lower case letters can be consolidated by playing games like *What's this?*, *Memory game* and *Bingo* (see Figures 8a–8h).

WORD RECOGNITION
As soon as children can recognise the lower case letters of the alphabet, flash cards of up to four whole words per lesson can be introduced. As their sight recognition of words expands, the number can be increased. The same method of introduction as for letters can be used, but as the word is read, the hand should move from left to right to indicate the word. It is useful to go over the cards a second time later in the lesson, if time allows, as this helps in learning.

1.3 Using flash cards

A large number of flash cards is needed for teaching and playing games. These can easily be made by the teacher.

Materials
Thick paper or thin card in light colours is best as the print shows up clearly. Where supplies are short, the inside of packets and old pamphlet covers can be used. Felt pen and ruler and pencil are needed for making guide lines for the letters.

Script

Letters approximately 3–5 cm in size so that they resemble as closely as possible the print in the first reader. It should be remembered that any uneven space between letters or words, or any badly made letter can be confusing for children in the initial stage of learning. For a detailed guide on how to make flash cards, see another book in this series *Look Here! Visual Aids in Language Teaching* (Bowen 1982).

READING RHYMES WITH FLASH CARDS

When children have learned all the flash cards of words in a rhyme they already know orally, they can arrange the flash cards on the floor or on their desk to 'write' the rhyme (see Figure 5). Having 'written' the rhyme using the flash cards, and having read the rhyme they have built, the children can then be given the text in the book, which they can read straight away. As they already know the rhyme, they quickly pass from reading word by word to reading the whole rhyme with correct stress and intonation, as well as meaning. Once children have learned to read three or four rhymes this way, they often teach themselves to read other simple rhymes which they already know orally.

Figure 5   Writing a rhyme with flash cards

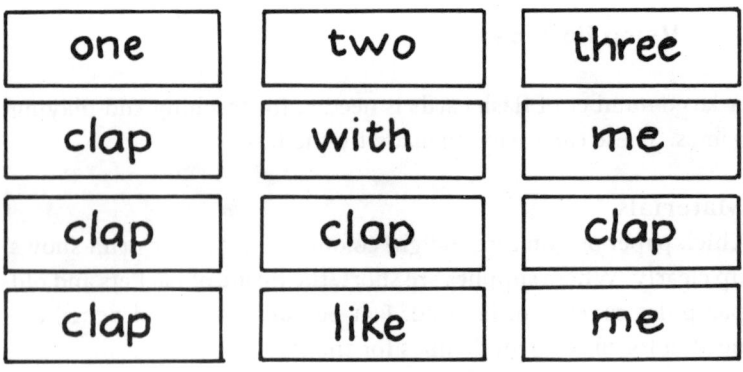

THE FLASH CARD GAME

The teacher puts a pack of flash cards, consisting of four cards of each of the words she is teaching, in any order face down in front of her. She picks up the first card, holds it up and says, 'Read this'. The first child to read it correctly takes the card. The teacher then picks up the second card and the game continues in the same way until all the cards are finished. She then asks the children 'How many cards?'. They count their cards, 'One, two, three', etc. The winner is the child with the most cards. The teacher then collects the cards asking first of all for all the cards of, for example, 'a dog' and then for all the cards of 'a bag'. As more words are learned, they are added to the pack. When the pack gets too big, the teacher selects the words which need the most consolidation.

MINI FLASH CARDS

Children enjoy having their own mini flash cards, made with print between 8 mm and 10 mm high. They can be used:

1 to play games in groups
2 to match with words in texts
3 to build rhymes
4 as cards in games like *What's this?, Snap, Bingo,* etc. (see Figures 8a–8h).

Using flash cards for a rhyme concert

Mini flash cards are very useful as they give children an opportunity to work at their own speed, thinking about what they are doing. Children need time to reflect when reading, as it is during this time that they work out their methods of decoding. For this reason it is essential to ensure that they are not exposed only to flash card work that demands quick responses. Individual work with mini flash cards also gives teachers an opportunity to check that children are not guessing words and really know how to read them.

Flash cards can be used until children have built up a reading vocabulary of between fifty and seventy words. By that time most children have acquired sufficient reading skill to read words they already know orally. In all cases flash cards should only be used for words children already know orally.

1.4 Reading books

Skill in reading, like all skills, takes time to develop and can only develop when learners are given many opportunities to read. Ideally, therefore, young children should find themselves in a reading-rich environment. This means that, in addition to their textbooks, they should have the chance to read some of the print around them in everyday life: posters, magazines and so on.

The following types of books are published for young children:

1 Rhyme and song books
2 Picture story books for Language 1 learners
3 Graded readers, for Language 1 learners (for example, *Ladybird* readers, *Language in Action* reading scheme)
4 Graded readers for Language 2 learners (for example, *Ranger* series)
5 Information books for Language 1 learners
6 Picture dictionaries for Language 1 learners

It should be noted that two types of graded readers exist. Those for Language 1 learners use a wide range of structures but are graded lexically so that they include only words within young children's interest and vocabulary. Within one page there is often a range of complex structures unsuitable for non-Language 1 learners. Graded readers for EFL/ESL learners may be abridged or simplified versions of well-known stories. They are carefully graded both lexically (in choice and number of words used) and structurally. Because of the tight control of language, some stories in such readers seem contrived in their use of language.

In selecting suitable readers for young beginners, the following points need to be considered:

1   Is the language contrived? Does it use natural English?
2   Is the story interesting for children? Is there a good story line?
3   What type of language control does it use – is it graded structurally, lexically, or both?
4   Are the technical details such as print size and type of illustration right for young beginners?

There are many beautiful picture books available in soft covers which, although not graded, use simple language which makes them suitable for young foreign learners. It is also possible for teachers to add their own texts to picture books which do not have words, in order to give children reading experiences right for their stage in English.

HOW TO USE BOOKS

The good easy reader consolidates vocabulary and uses it in such a way that the learner can give a greater width of meaning to words he already knows. When using readers, teachers should aim to practise language skills as well as to develop an ability to read for meaning and communication. Teachers may find some of the following activities helpful:

1   Read the story aloud. Where children are emergent readers, teachers can use the reading and pointing technique. As children become more skilled they can read together or read parts of the story for the teacher.

2   Talk about the pictures and relate them to the text.

3   Talk about the text and use of words.

4   Talk about the story.

5   Talk about the personalities in the story.

The teacher can devise her own workbook activities to be completed when the book has been finished. They should be based completely on the book and introduce no further material (see Figure 6 for an example).

As young children are not capable of writing book reviews, the teacher can ask them questions about the book which they can answer orally.

Another way of finding out how much children have understood and enjoyed a book is to ask them to make an additional illustration for the book or to make another book cover. When talking to them about their illustrations, it is possible to find out about their level of appreciation and understanding.

READING ALOUD (ORAL READING)

Reading aloud is a skill different from silent reading and children need opportunities to develop both. However, not too much importance should be put on reading aloud in a group, especially from a textbook or reader, unless there is a definite purpose. Reading aloud is not a skill many adults have to use. There is also the danger, when too much of this is done, that children are trained to scan only at the speed they can put the words into speech. In fact, efficient silent reading should be at a much faster pace.

However, young children to appear to enjoy reading aloud, especially to the teachers; they continually ask when it is their turn and are disappointed if they do not get a chance. Reading

Figure 6 Workbook activities

aloud seems to motivate and to give satisfaction; children do not seem to mind reading the same text over and over again, and each time they refine their performance. Reading aloud to the teacher also gives children an added opportunity to have personal contact with the teacher, and enables the teacher to hear any mistakes and evaluate the child's decoding techniques.

Children should never be expected to read aloud any material they have not already encountered orally. The material that is read aloud should be not only the textbook or reader, but also notices, lists, invitations and other material connected with activities taking place in the classroom.

Children learn from imitating, and if we want them to read well it is necessary for them to hear a good model of reading. Models can be either the teacher reading or a recording. However, for young children there is no substitute for the teacher and personal contact.

SILENT READING (AURAL READING)

Where children have their own copies of books, they can listen to the teacher or to a cassette and follow in their own books. Where a selection of story picture books are available, children can read silently at their tables or in the Book Corner (see Chapter 5).

COPYING (VISUAL READING)

Copying consolidates reading and opportunities for copying should be given either during the lesson or for homework. Children can copy texts from their story books or rhyme books, adding their own illustrations, which, apart from giving them opportunities to be creative, show the teacher the depth of their understanding of the text. They can also copy invitations, programmes and tickets for activities like puppet plays. Children enjoy making their own games, many of which involve copying material to make cards. Many of the games described at the end of this chapter are suitable for this.

In countries where no books are available, children often have to rely on what they copy from the blackboard. Where the writing on the blackboard is not very clear or children do not have good handwriting themselves, the copying is not always correct and sometimes children cannot read what they have written. In these circumstances children should have an opportunity to show their books to the teacher and read aloud what they have written to her.

CORRECTING MISTAKES

The skill of reading results from looking at a word and using the most relevant clues to decode it and give it meaning. Naturally children make mistakes. Goodman prefers to refer to mistakes or errors as 'miscues' (Gollasch 1982). A miscue is the divergence between the actual reading of the word made by the child and the correct reading. An analysis of the 'miscues' a child makes gives the teacher an insight into how the child is using his knowledge of clues to decode words.

In most cases, since at this stage children should always have encountered orally material they are asked to read, (and pictures accompany the text, providing important clues), children manage to correct their own mistakes, if given time. Often teachers and other eager children in the group supply the correct reading before the reader has had time to reflect. If children do not have opportunities to work out how to read by themselves, they cannot develop their own techniques. Self-correction is a means of allowing a child to develop his own system of decoding and the responsibility and independence of a mature adult, so it is important that the teacher does not intervene too soon and that she restrains the quicker ones in the group.

1.5 Reading difficulties

If a child is not making progress in reading and is gradually beginning to fall behind the others, it is important to find out the reason as soon as possible and take some action.

It may be that the child has not had sufficient opportunities to consolidate. If this is the case, a revision programme of flash cards and games is often sufficient to bring a slow reader up to standard. The stimulus of a different reading book or other new materials is often helpful, or some special responsibility in the classroom which involves reading.

The child may be having a problem in seeing or hearing which has not previously shown up. It is possible to test his sight by asking him to read letters and to test his hearing by saying things in a whisper behind him so that he cannot lip-read. If there is any suspicion that either his visual or auditory ability is not up to standard, a test by the school nurse or some other qualified person should be arranged. It is also advisable to check his scholastic ability in Language 1. If he is having learning difficulties (particularly with reading) in other classes, it is unreasonable to expect rapid progress in English.

If none of these explanations appears to answer the problems, it is advisable to discuss the matter with his Language 1 teacher and also with his parents.

1.6 Picture dictionaries

Aims of making a picture dictionary are:

1 to introduce children to using a dictionary by acting as a bridge to the first printed picture dictionaries
2 to introduce, in a realistic and meaningful way, the simplest relationships between the letters and sounds of the alphabet
3 to provide children with their own reference book for checking spelling.

Materials
Children need a plain notebook or drawing book allowing a double page for each letter. If notebooks are not available, children can make their own books using plain paper. Children can either cut objects out of magazines or draw their own. Entries can be made in one or two columns depending on the width of the page. The activity book by Abbs and Worrall (1979: 4) shows clearly how to make a picture dictionary. (See Figure 7.)

HOW TO MAKE 'MY PICTURE DICTIONARY'

Step one

Write a capital *A* and a lower case *a* in the top left hand corner of the first double page. Say: 'This page is for the letter *a* (/eɪ/). This is letter *a*. Its name is *a*.'

Continue labelling the pages in this way.

Step two

Select from the children's reading book two words beginning with the letter *b* and followed by a vowel, eg *ball* and *bag*. Draw the first object and label it *a ball*. Then say, 'This is letter *b*.'

Let the children say 'ball' several times until they get used to the sound. Then draw the second object. Including the article 'a' (pronounced /ə/) does not confuse children; however, teachers should generally avoid using the strong form /eɪ/ in pronouncing it.

Step three

Revise the words on the *Bb* page. Then introduce two more objects from the following consonants:

Dd   Ff   Jj   Ll   Mm   Nn   Pp   Rr   Ss   Tt   Vv

At this stage it is easier for the children if the consonants are followed by vowels. Continue introducing two objects in each lesson until all the above consonants have been introduced.

Step four

Introduce the following consonants in the same way:

Cc	*cat*	*Kk*	*king*
Gg	*garden*	*Qq*	*queen*
Hh	*hat*	*Ww*	*watch*

At this stage, avoid:

soft Cc as in *centimetre*

soft *Gg* as in *gentle*

silent *Hh* as in *hour*.

Step five

Continue to introduce objects beginning with consonants and gradually include some beginning with two consonants, for example:

sh	*ship*	*bl*	*blue*
ch	*chair*	*bl*	*black*
br	*brush*	*tr*	*train*

However, it is better not to draw children's attention to these combinations at this stage, though any discoveries they make should be confirmed.

Step six

Introduce initial vowel sounds pointing out that we call the vowels *a e i o u* but there are many different ways of saying them. They have different sounds (phonemes).

Begin by introducing the so-called short forms; after, introduce the so-called long forms. Point out that the long vowels often have the same name as sound.

Short vowels	*Long vowels*
a − ant, apple, ambulance	*a − apron*
e − egg, elephant	*e − eel, eagle*
i − insect	*i − ice*
o − orange	*o − open*
u − umbrella	*u − uniform*

Figure 7   A picture dictionary

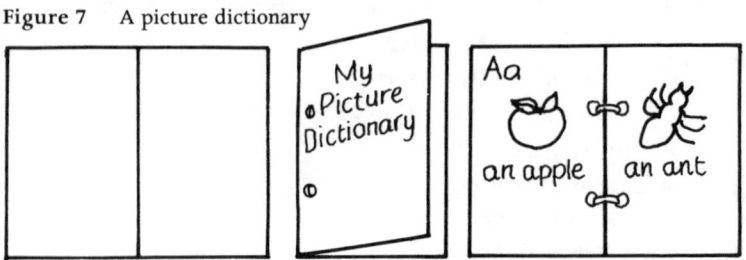

1.7 Games for consolidation

How to organise and play games is covered in Dunn 1983: Chapter 5. Another book in this series (Rixon 1981) also deals with using games. The following are useful for consolidating reading:

MATCHING

LEVEL Beginners
AGE 6-9
PLAYERS Individuals,
        pairs or groups
TIMING 5-10 minutes
LOCATION Outside/Inside
         (table or flat
         surface)

Aural/Oral/Reading
GAME LANGUAGE
What's this?
Read it / Read it to me
Is this the same?
No, that's not the same

MATERIALS Game cards with pictures and others with the corresponding word. Pictures should be very simple, illustrating only the written object.

DESCRIPTION The players are given a pile of picture cards and a pile of cards on which the corresponding words are written. The players arrange the pictures in a line and put the corresponding word under the picture.

DEVELOPMENT Develop the words into phrases, for example a cat in a bag, a cat in a basket, a dog in a car, a dog in a house, etc..
The same game can also be played with numbers.

Figure 8a

WHAT'S THIS?

LEVEL Beginners
AGE 6-9
PLAYERS Individuals in group
TIMING 5 minutes (can be
        extended to 10 if played
        in Stage 3 of lesson)
LOCATION Outside/Inside
          (a flat surface)
MATERIALS 5 cm square cards
           with pictures of a dog,
           a cat, etc. At least two
           cards of each object.

Aural/Oral
GAME LANGUAGE
What's this?
a dog, a cat, etc
It's a dog
It's a cat

DESCRIPTION The teacher shows the children picture cards telling them what each one is: 'a dog, a cat,' etc. She then places them face down on a table or flat surface. The teacher then points to a card and says, looking at a player, 'What's this?' The player guesses, for example, 'a cat', and picks up the card. If the guess is correct he keeps the card, if it is incorrect he replaces the card in the same place. The teacher then points to another card and asks another player. The game continues until no more cards are left. The player with the most cards wins.

DEVELOPMENT The game can begin with 2 pictures each of 3 different objects and gradually cards of other objects can be introduced. This game can also be played with alphabet cards, small letters and capital letters. Word cards can gradually replace picture cards.

a cat

Figure 8b

MEMORY GAME

LEVEL Beginners
AGE 6-9
PLAYERS Individuals in group
TIMING 5 minutes (can be
        extended to 10 if played
        in Stage 3 of lesson)
LOCATION Outside / Inside
        (a flat surface)
MATERIALS 5 cm square cards
        with pictures of a dog,
        a cat, etc. At least two
        cards of each object.

Aural / Oral
GAME LANGUAGE
a dog and a cat, etc
two dogs, etc

DESCRIPTION The teacher places the cards face down on a flat surface. The first player picks up a card and says, 'a dog'. He then picks up a second card and says, 'and a cat'. If the two cards are not the same he replaces them in the same places on the table. If the two cards are the same, the player then says, 'two dogs', and keeps the cards and has a second turn. The player with the most cards is the winner.

DEVELOPMENT Picture cards can be replaced by word cards, phrase cards and sentence cards.

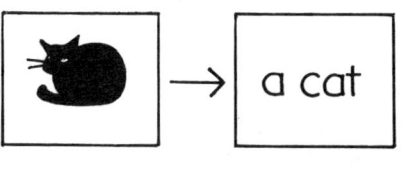

Figure 8c

SNAP

LEVEL Beginners
AGE 6-9
PLAYERS Individuals in group
TIMING 5 minutes (can be
extended to 10 if played
in Stage 3 of lesson)
LOCATION Outside/Inside
(a flat surface)
MATERIALS 5 cm square cards
with pictures of a dog,
a cat, etc. At least two
cards of each object.

DESCRIPTION An equal number of cards is given to each player, who places them in front of him face down. The first player turns over the top card, says what it is and places it at the side of his pile of cards, face upwards. The second player then does the same as the first player. If the cards are different the third player then turns over a card. If any two cards are the same, any player can shout 'snap'. The first player to shout 'snap' and say 'two dogs' picks up the two piles of cards and places them under his pile. If two players shout at the same time, the two piles of cards are placed one on top of the other in the centre. These cards are like another pile of cards and can be used for a snap. When a player finishes his pile of cards, he waits for an opportunity to call 'snap' and win some more cards. The game can finish when wanted. The winner is the player with the most cards.

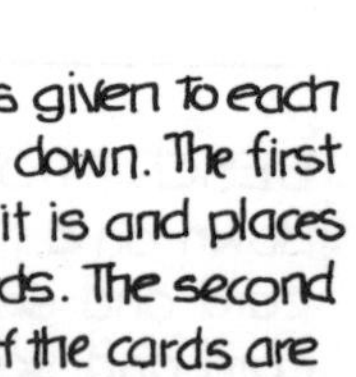

DEVELOPMENT Picture cards can be replaced by word cards.

Figure 8d

BINGO

LEVEL Beginners
AGE 6-9
PLAYERS Individuals in group
TIMING 5 minutes (can be
extended to 10 if played
in Stage 3 of lesson)
LOCATION Outside/Inside
(a flat surface)
MATERIALS Bingo boards made
of cardboard to fit
same cards as used
in WHAT'S THIS?

Aural/Oral
GAME LANGUAGE
I've got a dog etc

DESCRIPTION The teacher gives each player a board. The teacher holds up the first card and says, 'a dog'. Any player who has a dog puts up his hand and shouts, 'I've got a dog.' The teacher gives the card to the first player, who places it on his board. The teacher then holds up the second card. The game continues until one player has a complete board of eight cards.

DEVELOPMENT Picture cards can be replaced by word cards. Pictures can be made more complex; for example, 'a dog in a car', 'a fish on a dish', etc.

Figure 8e

TREASURE HUNT

LEVEL Beginners
AGE 6-9
PLAYERS All class
TIMING 5-10 minutes
LOCATION Outside/Inside
MATERIALS 12 numbered
cards and a small
treasure

Aural/Oral/**Reading**
GAME LANGUAGE
Look on the desk
Look under the table
Look in the bag
Look near the window

DESCRIPTION Numbered cards with written instructions are hidden. Players are told where to find card 1 (Go to the door). They follow the instruction and find card 2, read it and follow the instruction and find card 3. The game continues in this way until the last card which tells the players where to find the treasure.

Go to the door ¹

Go to the window ²

Figure 8f

GOING SHOPPING

LEVEL Beginners
AGE 7-9
PLAYERS Individuals in group
TIMING 5-10 minutes
LOCATION Outside/Inside
(circular area or table)
MATERIALS Picture and word cards of things to buy

Aural/Oral/Reading
GAME LANGUAGE
My mother is going to the supermarket
She wants a/some.....
and.....

DESCRIPTION Children sit in a circle or round a table. The first player begins by saying, 'My mother is going to the supermarket. She wants some apples.' The next child continues, 'My mother is going to the supermarket. She wants some apples and a chicken.' Children take it in turn to add on things to buy which can either be a/an or some. If children forget articles on the list, the other children can describe them using actions. The game finishes when the list is too long. Picture and word cards of things to buy are given to players before the game begins.

Figure 8g

HAPPY FAMILIES

LEVEL Beginners (readers)
AGE 6-9
PLAYERS Individuals in small
    groups
TIMING 10-15 minutes
LOCATION Outside/Inside
    (table or flat surface)
MATERIALS Cards for 5 families
    (4 cards per family),
    Cue sheet for each
    player

Aural/Oral/Reading
GAME LANGUAGE
Have you got.....?
Yes, I have
I've got......
No, I haven't
I haven't got......

Cue sheet

Mr. Brown. He's a doctor
Mrs. Brown. She's a teacher
John Brown. He's a schoolboy
Mary Brown. She's a baby
Mr. Smith. He's a policeman
Mrs. Smith. She's a housewife
Tom Smith. He's a schoolboy
Pat Smith. She's a schoolgirl

Cue sheet to include 3 more
families

DESCRIPTION The teacher gives out the cards to the
players. The players arrange their cards in families. If any
player has all four cards of one family, he puts them

Figure 8h

Mr. Brown
He's a doctor

Mrs. Brown
She's a teacher

John Brown
He's a schoolboy

Mary Brown
She's a baby

down on the table in one line. The players then try to collect families of cards by asking other players in turn, 'Have you got Mr. Brown? He's a teacher.' If the player asked has got the card, he replies, 'Yes, I have. I've got Mr. Brown', and gives it to the asker. The asker then has another turn and asks any player, 'Have you got...? She's .....'. If the player asked has not got the card he replies, 'No, I haven't. I haven't got ....' He then asks another player. The game continues until all the families have been put on the table. The player who has collected the most families is the winner. Players each have a cue sheet to help them with the language.
DEVELOPMENT Adding more families.

2 Beginning handwriting

Secret languages and codes seem to fascinate young children and possibly for the same reason many seem interested in being able to write English, which they see as another sort of 'code'. To write in English also provides written 'proof' of progress for both the child and his parents. This gives satisfaction that motivates.

Handwriting has to be taught carefully, following a graded programme, if young children who cannot write (or whose script is different from Roman script) are to learn quickly and with few faults.

Handwriting follows learning to recognise letters and words and most children can read written language before handwriting has been mastered.

As soon as children know and can recognise the small letters, they are ready to begin learning how to write them. Since the basic concept of what writing represents has already been learned, young children who can already write in their mother tongue (even if the script is different from Roman script and the writing direction other than from left to right) soon learn to write in English when presented with a structured programme. Since this is the situation for most teachers, the problems of beginning writing with children who cannot yet write in Language 1 are dealt with later in this chapter.

2.1 Introducing handwriting

Young children who already write Roman script find no difficulty in writing English and should be allowed to write either in print script as in the first reading and writing books, or in the same style as they write in Language 1. Many teachers have noticed, however, that some children who already write languages in cursive (joined) Roman letters choose to write English in print script in the early stages of learning.

Materials

Handwriting must flow easily; to obtain an easy flow it is essential that the writer has a light touch. To obtain such a touch it is necessary to use a pencil or writing utensil which requires the use of very little pressure to write. For this reason young children should be introduced to writing using a very soft pencil (2B) with a blunt point. Electric pencil sharpeners give a fine point, ideal for writing Chinese characters, but too sharp to obtain a smooth flow when writing Roman letters. As young children gain in skill they can move on to using a B pencil and eventually HB. It should be remembered that most ballpoint pens require a lot of pressure to get an even flow and are not advisable for writing in the habit-forming stage. Many other cheap disposable pens are too fine and pointed for beginners.

In countries where the handwriting system is different from Roman script, it is better to have a special pencil for writing in English. This helps children to make the transfer to the different handwriting system, which might also require a different way of holding the writing utensil. For example, some Japanese children hold a pen or pencil differently when writing Japanese than when writing Roman script, as different movements are involved.

RIGHT-HANDERS
Children who write with the right hand should place their paper slightly to the right-hand side of their body to facilitate movement from left to right. The paper should be placed parallel to the bottom of the desk, but as movement takes place it can become slightly tilted to the left. The pencil should be held lightly

between the thumb and first finger, about 1 inch (2.5 cm) from the point, with the middle finger providing additional support. The other two fingers can rest lightly on the paper. The pencil should be placed on the paper in a position between about ten and eleven on a clock, that is about 45° to the left of the upright (see Figure 9).

Figure 9   Handwriting points to check

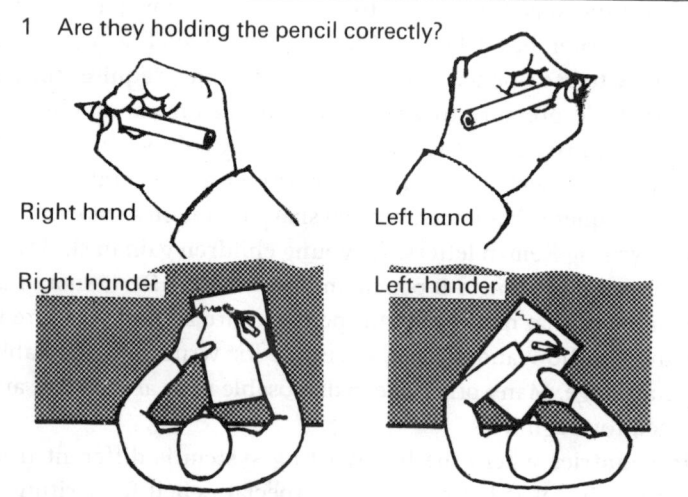

1   Are they holding the pencil correctly?

Right hand   Left hand

Right-hander   Left-hander

2   Are they sitting with their paper placed in the right position? (This is especially important if they are left-handed.)

3   Is their writing properly on the line?
4   Are the letters which go below the line the right length?
5   Are the tall letters the right height? (Remember *t* is not as tall as the others.)
6   Are they making the bar across the *t* and the *f* after they have made the down stroke?
7   Do they make the dot on the *i* after they have made the down stroke?
8   Is there a space the same size as a small *o* between their words? When they begin a word with a capital letter, do they write the following small letters close to the capital? (There should be no more space than between small letters in a word.)

LEFT-HANDERS

Children who write with the left hand should hold the pencil in the same way as right-handed children, except that the grip should be further away from the point to enable children to see what they have written, and the unsharpened end should point towards the body. This position helps to avoid the natural inclination of the left-hander to push the hand to write. The paper should be placed on the left side of the body at a steep slope towards the body in order to enable the hand to pull away from the writing (see Figure 9).

Other styles which, for example, involve placing the arm above the line and hooking the hand round to hold the pencil, which is used by some American left-handers, are to be discouraged as they make later speed writing difficult to achieve.

HANDWRITING SIZE

Young children cannot write letters as small as some adults can, as they do not have fine enough muscular control. To write them very large is also difficult for young children, as this also requires well-developed muscular control. For young children who already write Language 1 in another script, first handwriting should be 5 mm in size. Gradually, as children grow in competence, the size can be reduced to 4 mm in size.

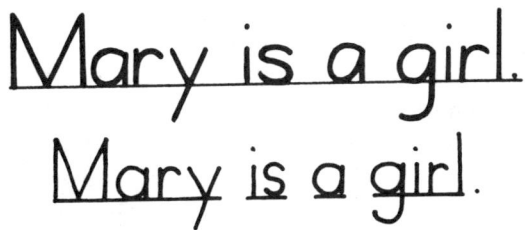

LINES

For young children whose writing is different from Roman script and who have little opportunity to see Roman script written by hand, it is very helpful to begin learning to write with four guide lines, as these lines help them to get used to the relative size and proportions of the letters.

Stop

Once young children have sufficient experience, the number of lines can be reduced to two and then one.

one girl

three girls

What do they have?

As young children become fluent in writing, they tend to use the one line as a base line to develop their own size of writing.

Young children seem to have none of the fears and apprehensions of older children about their skill in writing on unlined paper. After two or three efforts they manage surprisingly well writing in reasonably straight lines on plain paper, developing a natural feel for presentation and layout. Many young children appear to have an ability to estimate size and it is important in handwriting that opportunities are given for them to develop these natural skills of estimation and presentation. The example in

Figure 10 is by a nine-year-old Japanese girl used to writing from top to bottom of the page who learned to write using the structured programme in Figure 3.

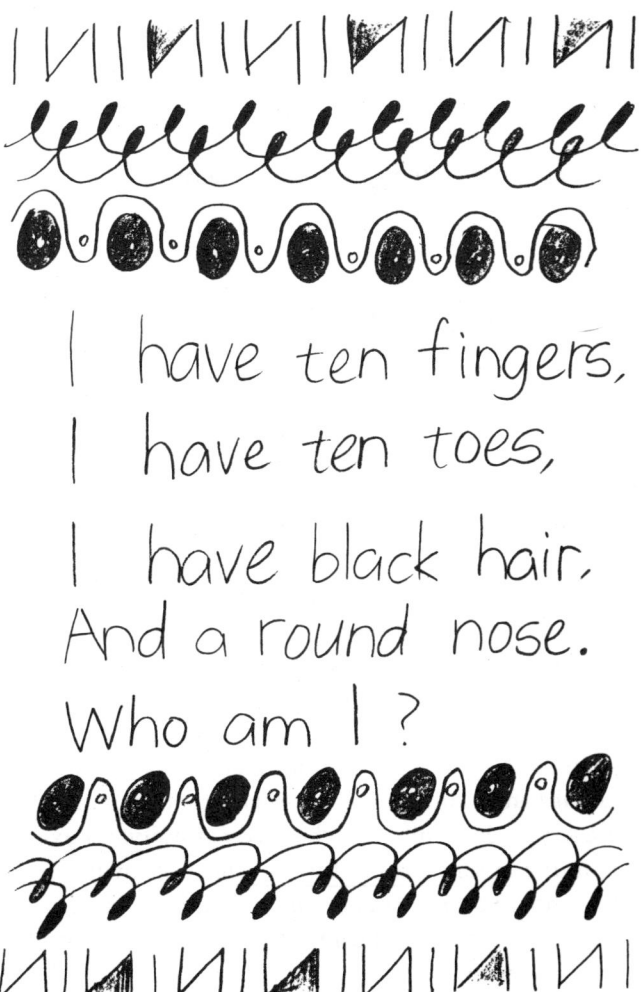

Figure 10   Japanese child's writing

2.2   Handwriting programme

Small letters (lower case) should be taught first, as they are most frequently written and read, and capital letters (upper case) second. Capitals are generally used only to fill up forms or attract attention on notices. If children are taught to write first in capitals, they naturally write their first words all in capitals. Once they have developed this habit it is, like all un-learning, difficult to break and words often get written like this:

Parents are often under the misapprehension that capitals are easier for young children to write. Teachers may find it advisable to explain to parents how they teach writing or even give them a copy of the alphabet they are using in order to avoid parents teaching differently from the school.

As soon as children know sufficient small letters to write words which they know orally, they should be encouraged to write them. When children have learned the capital letters, the capital letters can be introduced into writing naturally at the beginning of personal names and for the personal pronoun 'I'. As children get more advanced, capitals can be used naturally; for example, at the beginning of sentences or for the names of towns.

Letters should be made in the simplest natural way using as few strokes as possible and concentrating on natural movements of the hand, movements which children have made since they made their first scribble-like drawings on paper. These natural movements lead on quickly and easily to cursive (joined) writing.

STRUCTURED PROGRAMME FOR INTRODUCING SMALL LETTERS

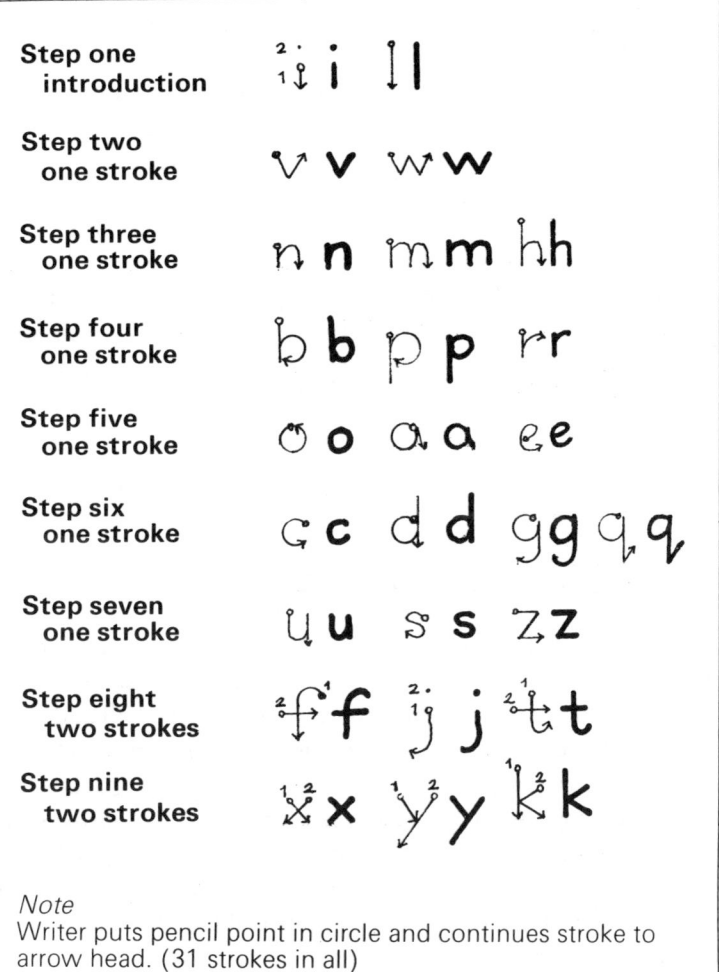

Step one introduction	ꞮꞮ i ǀǀ
Step two one stroke	ʋ v ꞷ w
Step three one stroke	ɳ n ɱ m ɦh
Step four one stroke	ƅ b ℘ p ꞃr
Step five one stroke	♡ o ɑ a ℮e
Step six one stroke	ᴄ c ɑ d ℊg ꞯq
Step seven one stroke	ʮ u ꞩ s ⱬ z
Step eight two strokes	∮f ꞌj j ⱦt
Step nine two strokes	x̌ x ẏ y ꝁ k

Note
Writer puts pencil point in circle and continues stroke to arrow head. (31 strokes in all)

Figure 11 · Structured programme for introducing small letters (print script)

The first step is planned to be very simple to allow the teachers time to check that each child has the correct pencil hold. Some children manage to achieve a surprisingly high standard of writing holding their pencil in unorthodox ways. However, if the writing utensil for writing Roman script is not held correctly, writing at speed, which becomes a necessary skill at a later stage, is difficult. If the correct habits of stroke order and hold are developed from the first lessons, later cursive writing develops naturally and quickly (see Chapter 5). As in most skills, learning faults acquired in the early stages of handwriting are difficult and time-consuming to eradicate.

Children want to use their knowledge of how to write letters to form words as soon as possible. After completing the first six steps above, they can write these simple words which they already know orally:

a dog a girl a car in
a man a bird on

Teachers should avoid making lower case letters by joining strokes, where, for example, an a is made from two strokes, a ball o and a short stick ı . This is an example of the 'ball and stick' method. It is difficult for some young children to make letters in this way as they have not, at this stage, fine enough muscular control to cope with the sharp movements, short strokes and accurate joins needed. At best, it can only be a temporary form of writing since later forms of cursive writing are based on continuous flow, which would entail making the letters using different movements.

After completing the nine steps of the structured programme, young children can write in small letters and should be encouraged to do so. However, the capital letters should be introduced as quickly after this as possible, following a graded programme. The use of capitals may be difficult for children who are not used to two sizes and forms for each letter. For example, Arabic, Japanese and Chinese do not have any comparable form.

STRUCTURED PROGRAMME FOR INTRODUCING CAPITAL LETTERS

2.3 Writing patterns

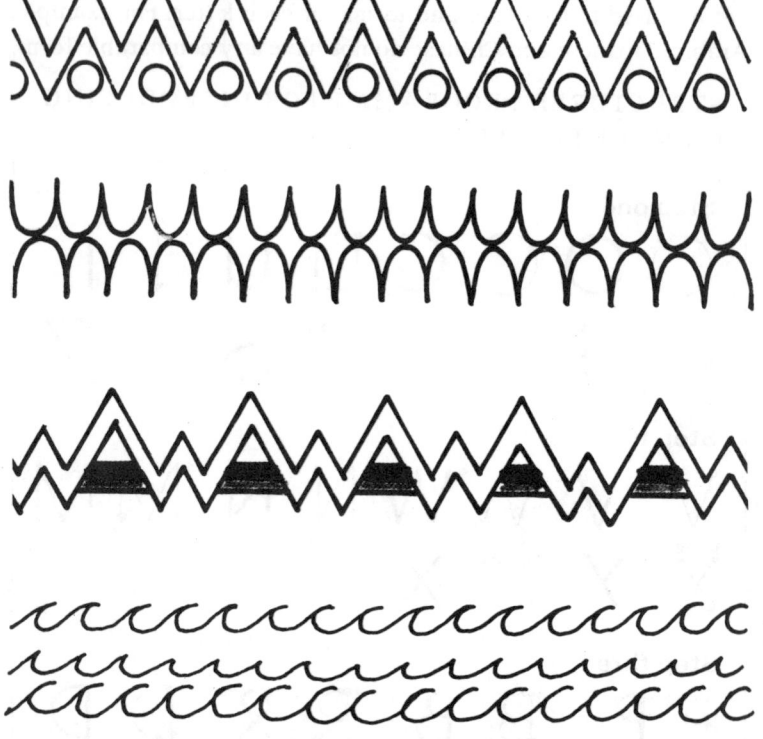

Writing patterns such as those above help children to develop the correct movements from left to right, to gain rhythm and flow as well as giving children opportunities to develop their natural ability to consolidate movements which are used in writing letters of the alphabet. Children appear to enjoy making writing patterns. Initially they copy patterns, but later build their own designs on to the basic patterns. Children who can already write in Language 1 are generally keen to know how to write the letters in English. For these children it is better not to delay the teaching of the letters by making writing patterns first as this may kill some of their enthusiasm. In these cases it is better to teach the letters and the related patterns at the same time.

Figure 13   Some practice patterns related to small letters (based on *Read and Write with Black and White Introductory Book*, Dunn 1979)

At a later stage children can be given opportunities to use writing patterns to decorate pieces of writing, cards, invitations, etc.

One two three
You can't catch me.
One two three
You can't see me.

Figure 14 Example of writing and pattern by a Japanese six year old

PREPARING YOUNG NON-WRITERS FOR WRITING

Young children who have not yet learned to write in Language 1 (non-writers) can be taught writing patterns (see Figure 15) as part of their reading/writing readiness programme. They can be encouraged to make the pattern in the air first and later transfer it to paper using either a thick wax crayon or paint brush. As they gain in muscular control they gradually transfer to using fat, soft pencils; pencil crayons are generally too hard for young beginners.

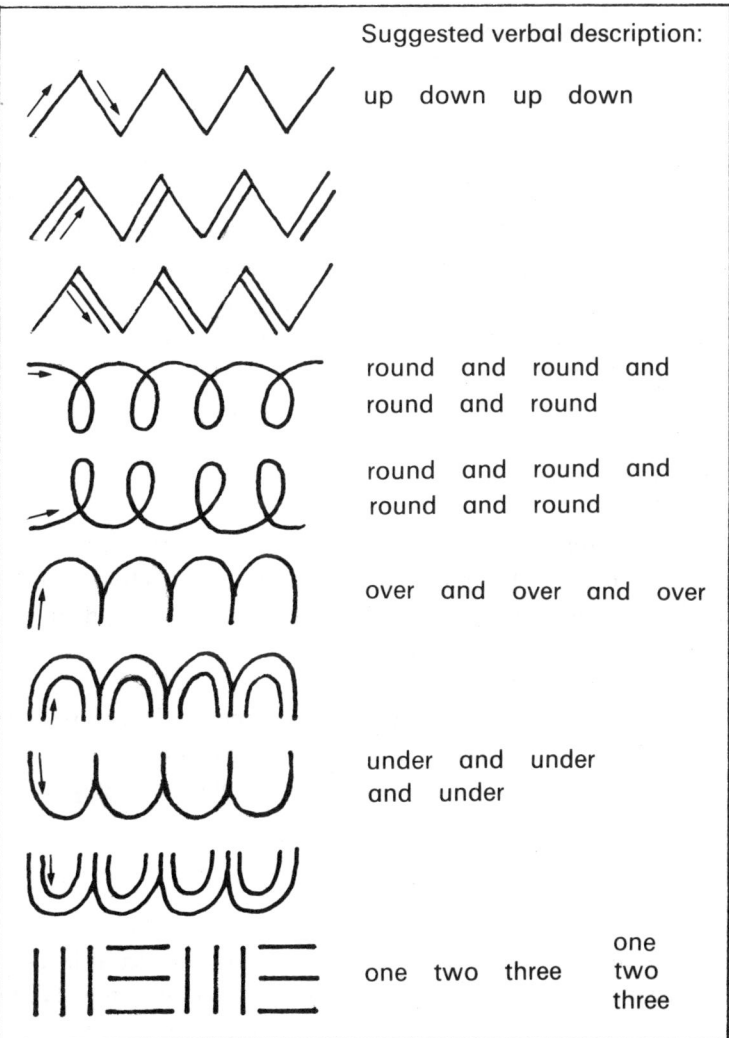

	Suggested verbal description:
	up down up down
	round and round and round and round
	round and round and round and round
	over and over and over
	under and under and under
	one two three one two three

Figure 15   Writing patterns for young non-writers

When children who cannot write in Language 1 are familiar with the basic writing patterns they can be introduced to the alphabet, letter by letter, following the grouping of the structured programme (see Figure 11). It is important that young children can see the demonstration of how to make a letter clearly – an overhead projector can be useful for this purpose. Children find it helpful if the teacher talks about what she is doing whilst making a pattern or letter. For example 'up and down' whilst making a pattern (Figure 15), or 'down and make a dot' whilst making an *i*.

Children often want to repeat what the teacher has said whilst making the pattern or the letter themselves. They frequently continue describing what they are doing aloud until they have internalised the process. For very young children a verbal description, as well as a visual and kinaesetic approach to writing seems necessary for successful learning. If possible, children should also be given the opportunity to feel the shape of letters – for this purpose sets of letters covered with nylon or felt are useful.

It is best for very young children to make patterns and letters on plain paper. The initial size of patterns and letters will be determined by each individual child's muscular development and degree of practice, and by the type of writing implement used (see Section 2.1 of this Chapter).

In the first instances children can copy from the blackboard. As they learn how to make letters, they can copy from writing cards which give an example of one or two letters and a related pattern.

2.4 Handwriting practice

Many young children enjoy doing some extra practice at home in the form of copying writing from rhyme books and even making their own anthologies, or copying stories. However, it is also essential that children use writing for communication purposes

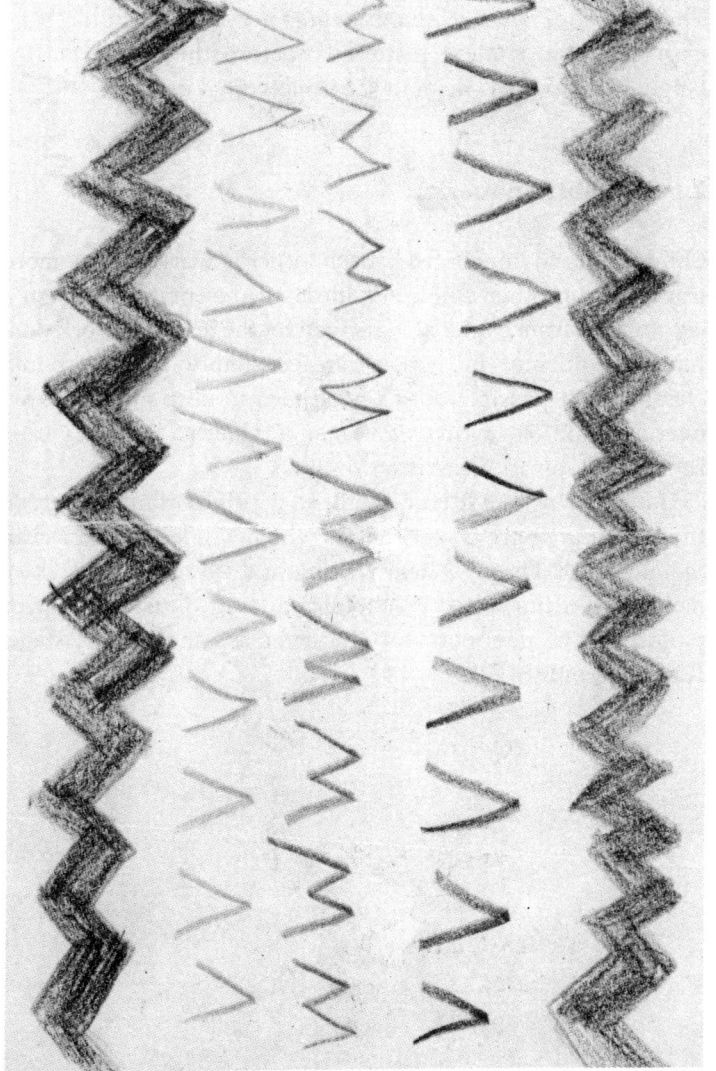

such as conveying messages or making invitations or programmes. Illustrations which accompany copying or writing at this stage are very important for the young language learner. They are equivalent to the drawings very young children make expressing their ideas pictorially before they have sufficient language to express them in the same verbal detail.

2.5 Exhibiting work

Children learn much from each other's work; often more is learned from other children's ideas of presentation, design and layout than from explanations given by the teacher. Work done at home or during the lesson can be simply displayed in the classroom. If possible, it is a good idea to keep children's work over a period of a term or a year in a folder so that they can see their development in writing skills.

Handwriting is a lifetime skill, so it is important to start from the beginning with correct habits which will lead on to writing a 'good hand'. Through handwriting and its related activities of making writing patterns, colouring and illustrating, young children have an opportunity for creativity in the early stages of learning English.

3 Beginning written communication

3.1 Copying

Once children know how to form letters and words, they are usually very proud of their newly achieved skill and want to use it. They may even use any free moments to copy out complete stories by themselves. It is best if their first experiences in writing English are in the form of copying, as this consolidates reading, reinforces the use of language items and helps learning to spell (see Section 3.5 of this chapter).

Young children enjoy copying writing from an example, especially if it has some purpose, like making cards for games, writing invitations, etc. It gives them a chance to reproduce something by themselves which does not need any correction by a teacher. It is also a creative experience for them, as handwriting in itself is a form of creative expression.

Copying can begin by writing names and words and, as oral ability and writing skills increase, can extend to phrases and sentences. As soon as children are capable, they should be encouraged to copy complete texts like rhymes and paragraphs from readers. Where possible they can add their own illustrations as, especially where texts are incomplete, the illustration adds what they cannot express verbally. Like native-speaking children, most young children learning English have greater oral than reading attainment. They can also usually read more than they can either copy or write by themselves.

Opportunities for copying can be given to children either during the lesson or as an extension of the lesson to be completed at home. As they have no time limit at home, they often spend a great deal of time completing this type of work. Figure 17 shows an example of copying based on a text from Dunn (1979: 10), where 'apples' have been transferred to 'oranges' (see also Section 3.2 of this chapter).

Figure 17 An example of copying and transfer in a child's homework

Good clear and consistent models are necessary if children are to be able to learn to copy correctly. Books which use print with a handwriting *a* and *g* are the easiest for children to copy from. Writing on the blackboard or on class notices needs to be clear and exactly like the print in books if consolidation is to take place and children are not to be confused. Any divergence from the basic shape of letters can be confusing for young beginners. Adults know from experience in reading different styles of handwriting, and from the position of a letter in a word, whether a letter is likely to be a *u* or an *n*; young beginners have not yet acquired this type of information.

AGE	11
GROUP SIZE	1
BACKGROUND	Language 1 = Japanese
SCHOOL	Japanese language primary school
	English EFL class outside school hours

This boy was being taught cursive writing in class. The only example of the writing was what he copied from the blackboard. As he was still learning a new script he sometimes made mistakes in copying; these were not corrected as the teacher did not look at the notebook. After six classes the boy had not understood the relationship between all the letters in his printed textbook and the cursive style of handwriting. When he copied from his textbook he continued to write a for *a* , g for *g* and capital S for *s*.

3.2 Transfer

As children's oral fluency increases, items of language can be transferred in part with the identifying word or words changed;

for example 'Put the book on the table' at the beginning of the lesson can be transferred to 'Put the pencil on the table' later in the same lesson.

Children can also be helped to transfer written work. So often textbooks are either about 'he' or 'she' and little help is given to children to transfer to 'I'. Young children generally want to transfer language and use it to talk about themselves since, at this age, they are very much concerned about themselves and their world.

Figure 18   Workbook activity (Dunn 1979: 39)

Children need to be carefully prepared for transfer, so that they can achieve it with a minimum of mistakes. Preparation can be done orally, using pictures for discussion as well as using mime. Written work should not be started until children feel confident that they know how to do it well. A sense of being able to do something well is in itself motivating.

After completing the workbook activity in Figure 18 (colouring the picture and repeating the writing), children can draw their own face and label it 'my face', 'my eyes', etc, using the workbook as a model. Further transfer can be made by playing the game *Touch your nose* (Dunn 1983: Chapter 5). In this game language could include 'Touch your nose. Don't touch your mouth.'

He is walking.
He is not jumping.
— — — ———
He is sitting down.
He is not standing up.
— — — ——— —

Figure 19   Workbook activity (Dunn 1979: 38)

After copying the writing in Figure 19 describing John's activities in the comic strip, children can make their own comic strip about themselves in the form of 'I am . . . . .' using the workbook as a model.

3.3 Text completion

As children gain greater oral fluency, they can begin to complete sentences and add missing words in carefully graded texts.

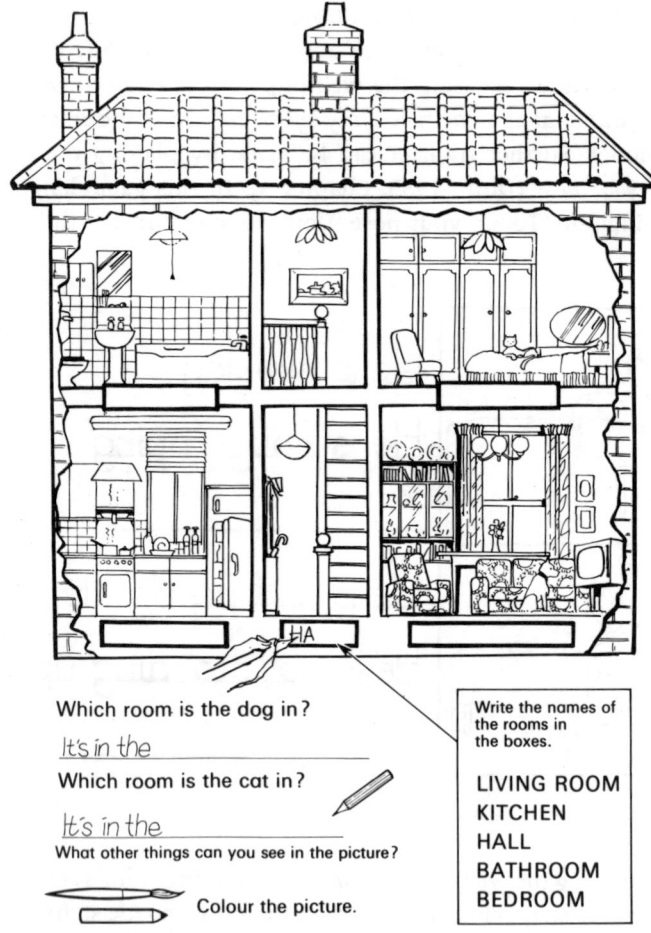

Which room is the dog in?

It's in the _____

Which room is the cat in?

It's in the _____

What other things can you see in the picture?

Colour the picture.

Write the names of the rooms in the boxes.

LIVING ROOM
KITCHEN
HALL
BATHROOM
BEDROOM

Figure 20 Workbook activity (Rixon 1980: 30)

After the workbook activity in Figure 20 has been completed, children can use the text as a model to help them transfer the text to accompany a picture of 'My house' or 'My flat'.

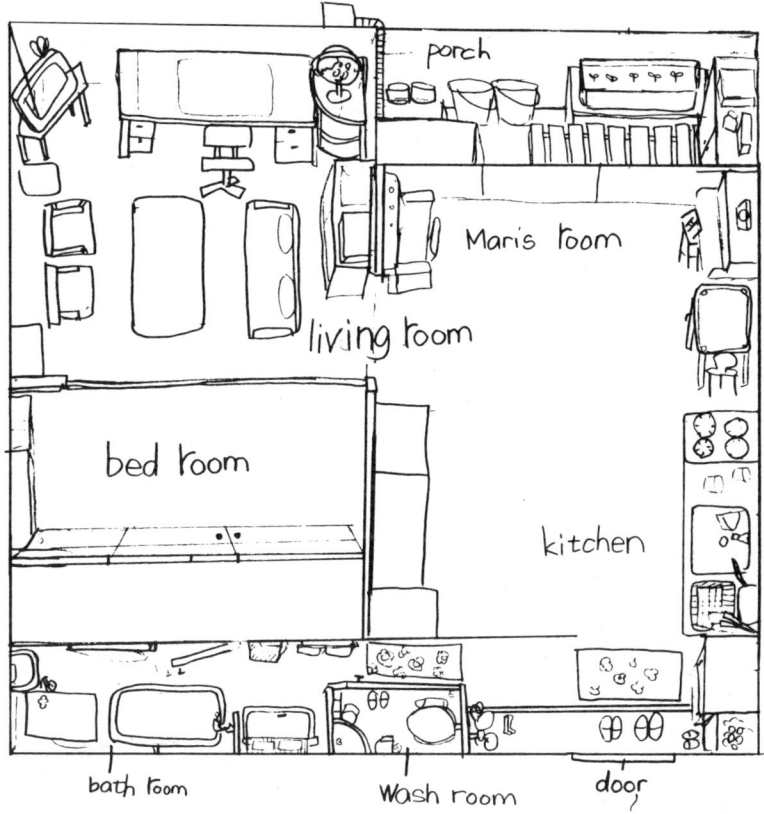

porch

Mari's room

living room

bed room

kitchen

bath room

Wash room

door

Figure 21   An example of transfer for 'My flat'

Personal use of written language can also be made after class discussion by putting together small individual books on subjects such as 'My family', 'My school', or 'My town'. These books can be simply made by stapling together four folded pieces of plain paper. In order to avoid mistakes in written English at this stage, it is better for teachers to provide the basic text for children to copy, page by page, into their books. Children can then illustrate each page themselves. Teachers can use these illustrations to stimulate discussion in English. Where time permits, teachers can talk to individual children about their illustrations and give them, as additional material for their descriptions of the picture, appropriate sentences arising from discussion.

Children can also make their own pictures or models of shops or houses, weather charts, etc, to which they can add written language. The content of the text can be worked out by the teacher and child together. The teacher can then write the text on a spare piece of paper leaving the child to make the fair copy himself.

A toy shop

A weather chart

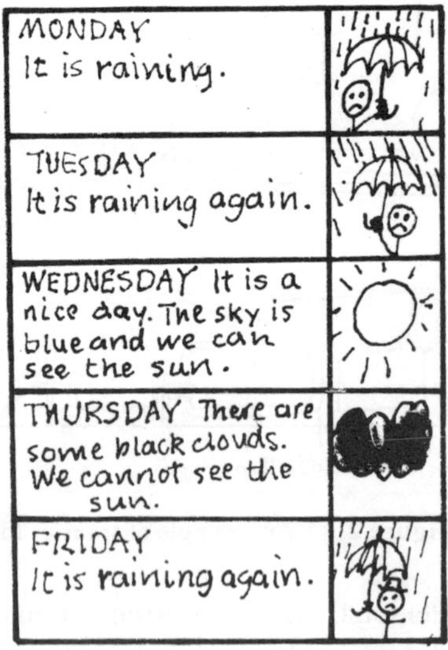

Note: Toys are cut out of a shop catalogue and put on the shelves with prices and labels.

Figure 22 Models for writing practice

This experience of copying and transferring leads on naturally to creative writing of simple texts and stories with the minimum of mistakes in Part Two (see Chapter 5). Where there are mistakes, however, they can be corrected in pencil by the teacher and then the work can be altered or re-copied.

3.4 Games involving writing

What is it?

It is small.

It is white and black.

It has four legs.

It has a tail. It has big eyes.

It has big ears. It can stand up.

It can sit down. It can walk.

It can run. It can not fly. What is it?

I know. It is a d o g

Figure 23 What is it?

After children have read the game in Figure 23 aloud, discussed it and guessed the answer, they can check their guesses themselves by completing the numbered diagram. This example can serve as a model on which children can base making their own games. This involves using the same structures but changing the descriptive words. For example, 'It is big' can be changed to 'It is small' and so on. As children get more used to doing this type of game they can add their own language items where relevant. This type of experience may lead on to story writing; it acts as a sort of bridge between copying and composition or creative writing.

Once children can use the simple past the same type of game can be used for recounting experiences. For example:

Yesterday I went to the toy shop and I bought . . . . .
It was big. It was red and white. It had two wheels. It had a bell.
What did I buy?
You bought a . . . . .

3.5 Spelling

When adults are not exactly sure how to spell a word in English they often write it down to confirm how it is written.

'Spelling is remembered best in your hand. It is the memory of your fingers moving the pencil to make the word that makes for accurate spelling.' (Nichols n.d.: 3). Children appear to remember the visual pattern of words, but in writing them consolidation takes place (see the following inset).

AGE	8
GROUP SIZE	1
BACKGROUND	Language 1 = Arabic Language 2 = French; an EFL situation
SCHOOL	French language primary school English EFL class outside school hours
LEVEL	At primary school writing in French and Arabic Reading English for two years with no writing practice

When she began to copy in a workbook she made many mistakes in copying simple words. With practice and encouragement from the teacher to look more closely at how words were made up, she corrected her mistakes, and her copying became quicker without faults.

To help children spell well, it is essential to give them regular opportunities to write words. After the first copying stage, once children are reasonably sure how to spell words, they should begin to write them without copying. Then books or picture dictionaries need to be available so that children can develop the habit of turning to them for reference.

3.6 Spelling games and dictation

Once children can read reasonably well they seem to enjoy easy spelling games. Apart from the practice these games give in listening, writing and actual spelling, they provide another quick activity in which children can use English in a natural situation. However, care has to be taken to ensure that the words which children are asked to spell are words which they know very well and have been asked to prepare beforehand. The choice of words should be such that every child in the class has a good chance of giving correct answers.

Most long words are best not spelt letter by letter as young children have difficulty in remembering a string of letters; if long words are broken up into syllables young children can count the syllables, which makes them easier to remember (see Dunn 1983: Chapter 4); for example:

walking	walk	ing	
going	go	ing	
football	foot	ball	
elephant	e	le	phant

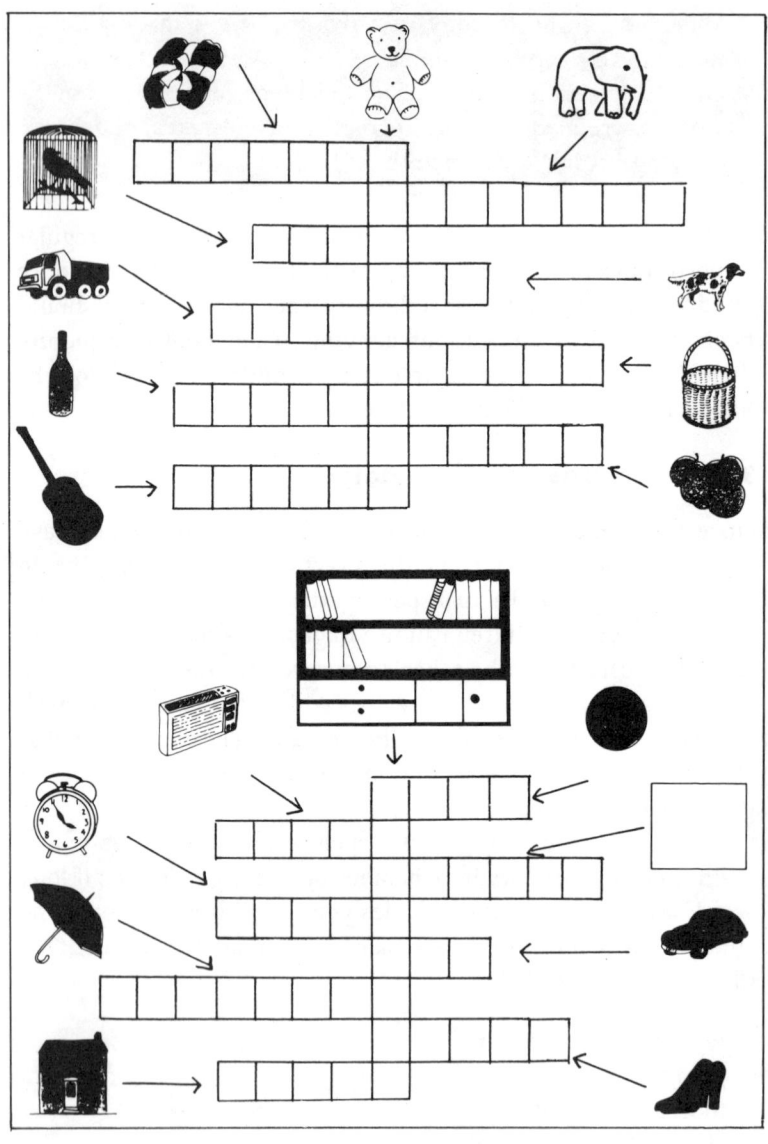

Figure 24   Crossword puzzle with pictorial clues (Byrne in Holden 1980: 39)

The temptation should be resisted to make the spelling games too difficult. It should be remembered that a game where all the children get all the answers right is not necessarily too easy. However, a spelling game in which more than a small proportion of the children produce wrong answers is too difficult.

A type of spelling quiz where children have their own small notebook in which they write five words selected by the teacher, is popular with children aged about seven and eight. The teacher discusses the words with the children and in reading them aloud slightly separates the syllables. Before the next lesson the children look at these words, probably copying them out once or twice. In the lesson either the teacher or another child dictates the words they have prepared, in any order, using them in simple phrases or sentences. Children then take turns at being the teacher and correct the spelling. Most children get all the words right each time, which gives them satisfaction and thus motivation. Any child who finds continual difficulty in spelling simple words correctly probably needs to be given more individual consolidation work. Simple crossword puzzles or game puzzles, with pictorial clues and using words which children already know how to spell or which they can look up in their reading or workbooks, are a good way of giving individual consolidation (see Figure 24).

Where the syllabus expects teachers to give beginners dictation, children should not be asked to spell words that they do not already know well. Young children do not have the wealth of experience that older children and adults have. Thus it is much more difficult to work out the sounds of words they have rarely either used orally or seen in written form.

4 Integrated language acquisition activities

Although school timetables and teachers divide learning into subjects such as history, natural science, etc, children do not compartmentalise learning in such a way. Similarly there is no division in young children's minds between oral and written communication in English – to them, listening, speaking, reading and writing are interrelated aspects of the same activity.

If lessons and schemes of work are planned around activities, integration of various aspects of language learning and consolidation takes place naturally. One of the most difficult parts of lesson planning is to select activities which are right for the children's level of development, and to use and sustain these activities so that they provide the maximum opportunities for communication. Activities of the sort described in this chapter normally take place towards the end of a lesson or in Phase Three of a lesson framework (see Dunn 1983: Figure 4, page 27), after introduction of new language related to the activity and consolidation of language have taken place.

At the beginning of Part One of a syllabus, creative language is less used and developed than prefabricated language (see Dunn 1983: Chapter 1 for this distinction). By the end of Part One, and as creative language develops, prefabricated language is less used in activities except for socialising and organising (see Dunn 1983: Figure 1, page 4). The following examples show, in detail, how activities have been developed for maximum language acquisition and communication. They use both prefabricated language and creative language. The balance between the amount of the two kinds of language depends on the stage of learning and the nature of the activity.

4.1 Stories

A story can be the starting point for various activities; for example, reading, writing, drama, handwork, etc. However, stories have to be carefully selected, as some do not give rise to many related activities and are difficult to act. Stories should not be chosen if they have too difficult lexis or structure, are too culture-specific or are unsuitable in subject matter.

Stories can be written in several ways. Narrative-style stories are interesting for children but do not give them enough of the language they can use for communication, which is what they want and need at this beginning stage of learning. Stories which are written in dialogue form are better as they can use the language with little or no change. *Go* picture readers are an example of this type of story. *Ranger* Story Workbooks provide readers with everyday spoken language in a dramatic reader which can be used for puppet or end-of-term shows.

Stories which are based on folk tales are very popular with children; they also include natural repetition which provides a type of pattern practice. In the story of 'The Three Bears', for example, all actions are done first by Father Bear, then by Mother Bear and finally by Baby Bear. The Story Workbook *Red Hen's Cake* (Dunn 1979) demonstrates how a story can be used as a base for different activities. This story is broken into units of one page on which there is text and an illustration of the action which takes place in the written text. The drawing is based on a child's visual interpretation of the text. The print used is the same as in first print handwriting, which makes copying easier. The picture has been adapted for colouring in order to provide an activity related to the text.

Red Hen   Here's the sugar.

Pig   What are you doing, Red Hen?

Red Hen   I'm making the cake.

Pig   Oh, you're making the cake.

Red Hen   Can you help me?

Pig   No, I can't. I'm sorry.

Figure 25   *Red Hen's Cake* (Dunn 1979: 15)

INTRODUCING A STORY

First stage (the teacher only with a book)

Step one
Introduce the main characters of the story using pictures, gestures and, if there are animals in the story, any associated noises.

Step two
Tell the outline of the story using the pictures and a selection of the key story-line sentences.

Step three
Retell the story in more detail using the pictures.

Step four
Retell the story introducing some of the language which children repeat with the teacher.

Step five
Retell the story as Step Four adding more language from the story text.
Introduce words of the first page of the story using flash cards.

Second stage (the children are now given their own copies of the book)

Step six
Introduce the first page of the text, children read the text and colour the picture.
Introduce the words on the second page of the story using flash cards.

Step seven
Introduce the second page of the text, read and colour.
Revise the first page of the text.
Introduce the new words on the third page of the story using
flash cards and consolidate all flash cards by playing the
Flash Card Game (see page 19).

Third stage

Towards the end of the story introduce the cassette and let
the children follow the story in their books whilst they listen
to the cassette. By this stage most children know the story by
heart.

4.2 Dramatic activities

Teacher and children acting *Red Hen's Cake*

PLAYS

If children have enjoyed reading or listening to a story, most of them already know it by heart. This makes acting it very easy for them.

Plays can be acted in groups. In some cases the teacher may find it helpful to play the leading role as it enables her to set the standard she wants. It also encourages the children greatly and makes for a very happy relationship between the children and teacher. Plays can either be acted in the classroom during the lesson, or, using props and costumes, as an end-of-term or end-of-year play. Parents and other classes, especially younger classes, always enjoy watching children they know act.

PUPPET SHOWS

Puppets can be made very simply using paper bags or faces made from cardboard and stuck on to lollipop sticks or wooden chopsticks (Dunn 1983: Figure 8, page 57). Story Workbooks and

Figure 26   Examples of simple stages for puppet shows

other workbooks often provide outlines of puppets for children to cut out and mount.

Shows can be given by individual children at home to the rest of the family or by pairs or groups to other children in either the classroom or the playground.

Stages can be made by using the back of a chair, using the edge of a table top or even an old television frame (see Figure 26). Children at this age do not seem to require any props when giving a show; speaking the parts (often changing their voices for characters with amazing skill) and moving the puppets seems to be sufficient to create the right atmosphere.

Some teachers are disappointed when shows do not reach the perfection they had hoped for. However, it should be remembered that the educational value of the show lies not in the final performance, but in all the preparatory work.

4.3 Invitations, programmes and tickets

Invitations to shows can be made by children for parents, teachers and other classes. This gives real significance to writing. Receiving and reading the replies is always an exciting experience in communication.

Children can also make their own programmes and tickets for use at shows. This kind of project, if well planned and organised, can integrate oral practice with reading and writing.

```
— Programme —
Red Hen's Cake

Red Hen ~~~~~ Edwina
Pig ~~~~~~~ Abdelhamid
Duck ~~~~~ Miriem
Cat ~~~~~ Imane
5 chicks    ~~ Yasmine
            ~~ Yan
            ~~ Ihsan
            ~~ Nadia
            ~~ Houda
```

```
Ticket 22 (twenty-two)
        for the
    Puppet Show
      in the hall
at 2 o'clock    On Tuesday
```

4.4 Cassette recordings

Step one
Children are given parts and prepare for the recording by reading or listening to the cassette at home or at school.

Step two
During the next lesson they record several pages (the complete text takes too long to record in one lesson).

Step three
The recording is then played back. Children tend to be critical of their own performances and like an opportunity to discuss how to improve.

Step four
After this discussion children then record again. If time allows they listen to the new recording. The children continue recording in this way.

It is interesting to notice how children manage to improve their pronunciation and general standard of reading from one recording to the next. Sometimes the standard of the cassette they make is so good that it can be used in other classes or on the school loudspeaker system as part of an English show or programme.

4.5 Handwork or art

Children can paint pictures to show the most important stages in the story, making a picture strip story. The teacher can then discuss with them what they would like her to write under the story. In most cases the teacher finds that she has to edit the children's language to make it into a simple, flowing story.

Where the story tells about making something as in the case of *The Gingerbread Boy* or *Red Hen's Cake*, the experience is completed by the children themselves making for example the cake, in the classroom or at home with mother. In the Story Workbook *Red Hen's Cake* the instructions for making the cake are set out in simple language at the end of the book. This has meant that many mothers have worked out the instructions in English with their children at home and produced a cake. In some classes this cake has become the cake which each child brings to school on his birthday.

Where activities are not suggested by or do not naturally develop out of the material being used by the class, or where opportunities for additional language practice are required, the teacher has to devise them herself. Below are some examples of activities that can be 'stage-managed' to generate opportunities for controlled yet natural communication.

TALKING ABOUT PICTURES

It is possible to obtain colourful posters and pictures from magazines, advertisements, airline publicity material, holiday tour brochures, etc (see Bowen 1982, for addresses and further ideas). Even black and white newspaper photographs of things like zoo animals, spacecraft and advertisements for new makes of cars, etc are interesting to children.

These pictures can be displayed on the classroom wall, stuck in a large book which children can look at each week, or stuck on card to make a large type of flash card. This can be used for many purposes including games.

The teacher can introduce one picture each lesson, discussing the picture with the children, stimulating language by asking questions such as 'How many cars are there? What colour are they?' At a more advanced level teachers can ask questions which require children to make some prediction, for example, 'What is the man going to do?'; or questions which involve recounting past events, for example, 'Where did he go yesterday?'. Care should be taken to avoid too frequent use of questions which only require a 'Yes' or 'No' answer, as these are less useful in stimulating thought and communication.

Even if children are not yet readers it is useful to write the name under the picture, for example, *a panda*. For children who can read (depending on the reading level of the class and the language the teacher wants to present or consolidate) this may be expanded to *This is a panda. He is in the zoo. He is black and white*. It is a good idea before introducing a new picture card to go through some previous cards as a consolidation exercise.

Some children might like to collect their own pictures. These could be stuck into a class book or children could make their own individual books. Depending on whether the children can read, the teacher can write or let the children copy a suitable description under the picture. Books like these can be kept in the Book Corner (see Chapter 5), as other children enjoy looking at things made by their classmates.

4.6 Making collections

Young children between the ages of seven and nine enjoy making collections of things. This interest in collecting can be used in activities in the English lesson.

Many children enjoy collecting bottle tops. Teachers can make use of this in the first lessons by asking them to bring their collections to school. This can lead on from individual counting to making charts showing how many each person has, how many the whole class has and who has the most. Some children enjoy showing off their knowledge of their particular hobby; some have their own collections of toy cars or animals, stones, stamps, etc. The teacher can ask them to bring them to school and the class can make a small exhibition of them. They can label them, discuss them and even invite other classes to come and see them by sending invitations or making posters which they put up round the school.

In any country, but particularly where the writing script differs from English, children can make lists of any words written in English; for example, international traffic signs, shop names, names of imported foods, etc. They can also collect labels of products written in English and stick them on a wall frieze.

4.7 Celebrating festivals

Local festivals are important occasions for young children and they often want to be able to talk about them in English. However, the necessary vocabulary is rarely found in books suitable for young beginners. For this reason it is advisable for teachers to make the material with the children. For example, for Carnival in Brazil they can make costumes; for the Easter Procession in Malta and Spain they can make pictures and friezes of the events; for the Feast of Saint Nicholas in Holland and other countries they can make gifts, write letters and decorate the classroom. Other international festivals can be introduced by talking about a related picture or pictures, eating some of the typical food or playing a typical game.

5 Beyond the beginnings

Part One of a syllabus (Dunn 1983: Chapter 2) is concerned with giving young children opportunities to acquire sufficient basic language for activities to take place using only English in the classroom. As the type of activities that take place in young children's classrooms are often very similar whatever the learning circumstances, the basic core of what children need to acquire is also more or less similar. Once they know and can use, for example, games language, organising language, language for activities, etc, courses begin to be more orientated towards the particular teaching situation of, for example, an ESL, EFL or bilingual school.

For convenience the basic core can be considered as Part One of a programme. Part Two can be considered as beyond the basics, when the orientation towards the learning situation becomes necessarily greater.

By the time children have completed Part One they are no longer beginners. They are post-beginners. They can manage to communicate in simple English in a variety of classroom situations and begin to use English to predict into the future and to recount past happenings. By this time they are also more mature; chronologically they may be several months or years older depending on whether they have been learning English in an English medium, or a bilingual school, or in a class as a foreign language. Children can now work at a more advanced level conceptually, physically, socially and emotionally. Their progress in both English and Language 1 will have contributed to this all-round development, enabling them to acquire more new language and consolidate it more quickly than in the early stages of Part One.

Language programmes should now concentrate on:

1 introducing more creative language so that creative language predominates
2 revising prefabricated language and introducing different ways of saying the same thing, so that children can begin to select the most appropriate language to use
3 revising the syllabus and introducing concepts which were too difficult or unnecessary for Part One
4 introducing further techniques in reading and handwriting.

5.1 Planning lessons

In Part Two children should still be able to acquire language through activities. A Part Two classroom has much the same feel and look as a Part One classroom except that activities are going on at a more mature level, requiring more advanced language and including more reading and writing.

The same basic lesson framework (Dunn 1983: Figure 4, page 27) can still be applicable especially in EFL classes. However, the length of the phases of a lesson differs from that in Part One in that the oral introduction of new work can now be shortened. Social greetings and goodbyes are still important whether at the beginning or end of a lesson, session or day.

ACTIVITIES
Children's greater maturity and fluency (both oral and written) widens the scope of activity in which they are able to take part. This is illustrated by the example of activities based on stamp collecting (see Figure 27).

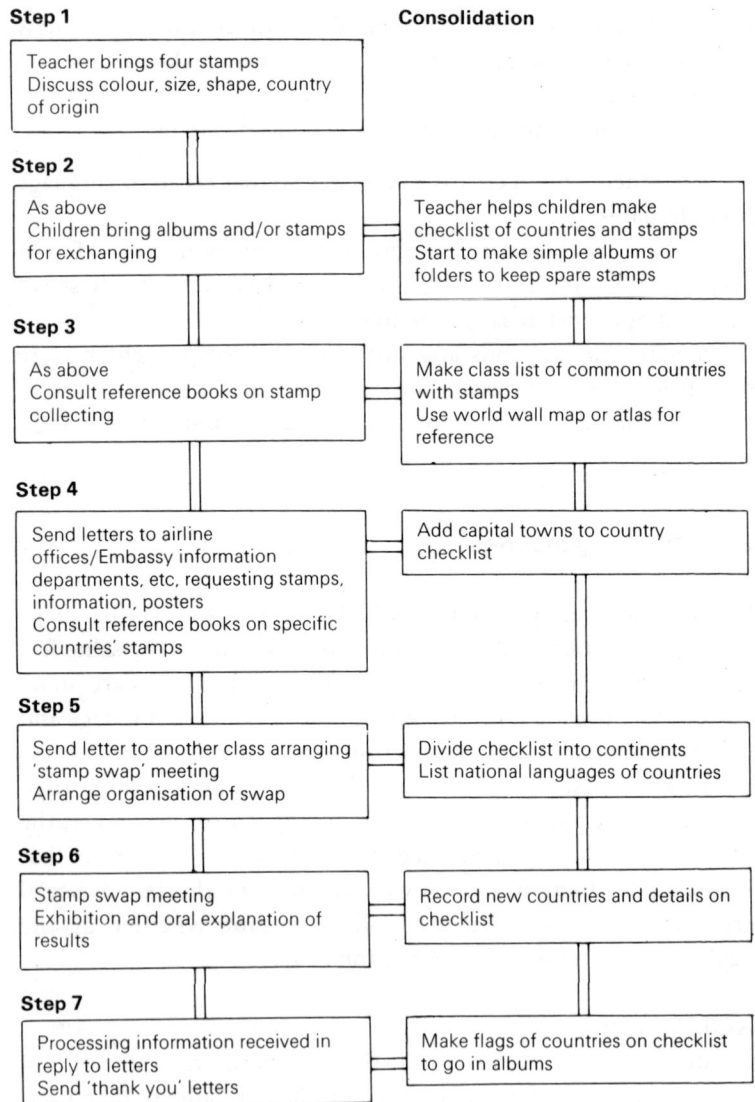

Step 1

Teacher brings four stamps
Discuss colour, size, shape, country
of origin

Consolidation

Step 2

As above
Children bring albums and/or stamps
for exchanging

Teacher helps children make
checklist of countries and stamps
Start to make simple albums or
folders to keep spare stamps

Step 3

As above
Consult reference books on stamp
collecting

Make class list of common countries
with stamps
Use world wall map or atlas for
reference

Step 4

Send letters to airline
offices/Embassy information
departments, etc, requesting stamps,
information, posters
Consult reference books on specific
countries' stamps

Add capital towns to country
checklist

Step 5

Send letter to another class arranging
'stamp swap' meeting
Arrange organisation of swap

Divide checklist into continents
List national languages of countries

Step 6

Stamp swap meeting
Exhibition and oral explanation of
results

Record new countries and details on
checklist

Step 7

Processing information received in
reply to letters
Send 'thank you' letters

Make flags of countries on checklist
to go in albums

Figure 27 Possible planning and development of an activity: stamp
collecting

In selecting activities the following general points may be applicable for Part Two:

1   Children are now ready to think beyond the immediate 'here and now' to the future and the past.
2   Children are ready to think beyond themselves and their way of life and are interested in the way other people live.
3   Children's interests have developed and many are collectors of stamps, fossils, miniature cars, etc.
4   Children are able to concentrate for longer periods and are therefore better able to fit into an activity.
5   Children are able to read and write and can thus find information from books and communicate with others by writing.
6   Children are better informed about their cultural background.
7   Children are less dependent on the teacher for sustaining activities. They enjoy working in groups with a group leader or in pairs.
8   Children are able to talk amongst themselves in English and can have simple discussions.

CONSOLIDATION

Without suffucent opportunities to consolidate, children can acquire language but not be able to use it effectively. Opportunities to consolidate orally and through reading and writing have to be planned into each lesson and individual children's progress has to be monitored.

MOTIVATION

For various reasons post-beginners often begin to lose interest in learning English and thus motivation is vital. Activities which are right for this stage of development and which are properly consolidated give children a feeling of success which in turn motivates. By Part Two children can motivate each other by using English in the classroom to talk about their work, their exhibitions, etc. The following are possible sources for activities at this level:

1 School English magazines
2 School English radio programmes (using school loudspeaker systems)
3 Joint class exhibitions, plays, etc
4 Local school English festivals, exhibitions, etc
5 Contact with English-speaking schools or pen friends
6 Visitors from English-speaking countries or from their own country who have to use English in their work; for example, an air hostess or a scientist
7 Visits to places where English is spoken; for example, a travel bureau, an airport, a frontier town, an international railway booking office, etc
8 Use of audio-visual material, especially video

5.2 Oral and written communication

'Language competence grows incrementally through an interaction of writing, talk, reading and experience' (The Bullock Report 1975: 515). Although this was written with reference to children whose Language 1 is English, it is also applicable to children whose Language 1 is not English.

By this stage there are opportunities for both oral and written communication within activities. It is no longer necessary for new language to be introduced orally several lessons before children encounter the written form. However, the teacher is still the only person introducing new spoken language (apart from visitors and audio-visual material), and for this reason teachers should continue to plan input carefully.

Children's oral ability should now be sufficient for them, once a pattern has been set by the teacher, to take over running some activities themselves. When children run activities, it is a good idea for the teacher to take part playing the role of a child.

Children's writing ability should by now be sufficiently fluent for more written activities to be included in the programme. Some children are ready to begin creative writing and a good way to start is by asking children to add a written description to a drawing they have made of, say, a family outing, a joke, etc.

Bearing in mind the possible sources of activities at this level (see Section 5.1 of this chapter), teachers might find the following useful for encouraging the skills of listening, speaking and writing:

1   Listening (aural) comprehension activities can include following the teacher's instructions on how to complete work sheets, playing games or completing tasks given on a cassette.

2   Dramatic activities can now include playing the roles of real people speaking English, for example a shopkeeper, (whereas in Part One dramatic activities are much more restricted).

3   Writing activities can include descriptions giving cultural and geographical information, enquiries seeking information about other countries, letters, diaries, book reviews (for Book Corner see Section 5.4 of this chapter), etc.

5.3   Further reading activities

By now children have a good basic sight vocabulary which has been built up from reading experiences. They are capable of using this vocabulary to read simple texts composed of words they have already encountered. Some children will have worked out their own method of decoding words; others will still find difficulty in reading unfamiliar words. In various types of activities they will have had practice in oral, aural and visual reading (see Section 1.5 of Chapter 1).

In Part Two the teacher needs to plan activities to increase children's reading skills in three areas: oral, aural and visual.

Where possible oral reading should take place in meaningful situations like play reading to make a cassette recording, reading out notices, etc. Opportunities for aural reading should be increasing, and children should begin to read for information or merely to skim a text. Visual reading opportunities should also increase in Part Two. A Book Corner (see Section 5.4 of this chapter) gives material for the practice of all the reading skills.

Each child's reading should be regularly monitored either once a week or once a fortnight depending on the frequency of the lessons. Teachers need to record children's progress and difficulties and check that every child has opportunities in the three types of reading.

In Part One (see Chapter 1) children were given some training in sound/symbol relations through:

1 rhymes and other forms of word play
2 breaking words into syllables for spelling activities
3 learning names and sounds of initial consonants and short vowels.

Other sounds can be introduced by continuing work on the picture dictionary (see Chapter 1) using words within children's oral vocabulary. Sounds can be consolidated by playing games using sounds. Games which children make themselves are often more meaningful than ready-made games and give the children the opportunity to talk about and write the sounds (see, for example, Figure 28).

Some good phonic readers which use language in a natural way can be added to the Book Corner (see Section 5.4 of this chapter). Examples of this type of reader can be found in the *Language in Action* series (Morris et al. 1974). Some teachers are very keen to introduce children to the phonic rules in a systematic way, imposing lists of words with the same sounds to be copied and learned. Young children find this systematic approach difficult as it is not within their experience in reading and learning.

AGE	9
GROUP SIZE	10
BACKGROUND	Language 1 = Japanese; an EFL situation
SCHOOL	Japanese language primary school
	English EFL class outside school hours

The teacher gave the children a long list of words to be learned for their phonic value for homework. In the next lesson she gave a test to see how well the children could write the words. Most of them got nearly all the words right. A few weeks later they were asked to use some of the words in a piece of writing. A large number of the children had forgotten how to spell them, as they had been learned as isolated examples for the test and not learned within a context which showed how and when the word was used.

In any work the teachers should remember these points:

1 Most phonic schemes have been written for Language 1 children and for their degree of oral reading fluency. Many include words irrelevant for young EFL, ESL beginners.

2 Some phonic schemes are not based on modern linguistic research.

3 Any change in accent of the model speaker whilst children are learning phonics can be disastrous. For example, a change from an American to a Scottish teacher can be confusing even for Language 1 children.

In enthusiasm for teaching the techniques of reading, teachers should not lose sight of the fact that reading is a means to an end, not an end in itself. It is a way of conveying and obtaining meaning and information. Reading skills should be acquired principally by this process rather than by focusing too strongly on non-natural, mechanical means such as systematic lists exemplifying the same phonic sound. Above all, reading should

Snap (with rhyming words)

house
mouse

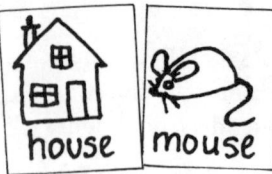

Examples:
(2 cards made for each word)

bank tank
sand hand
ring sing
fish dish
pan man
rain chain
box fox
big pig
sun bun
bell shell

Happy Families

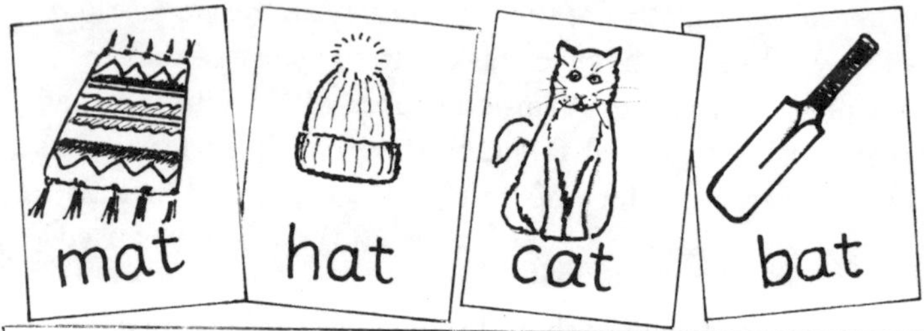
mat
hat
cat
bat

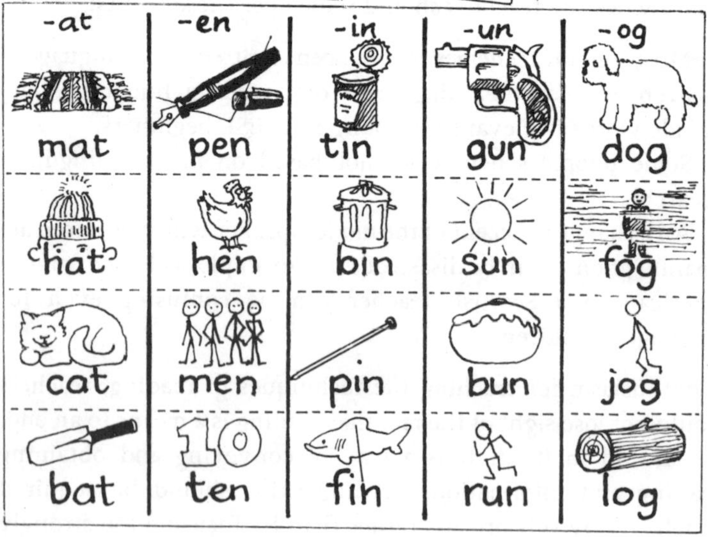
-at
-en
-in
-un
-og
mat
pen
tin
gun
dog
hat
hen
bin
sun
fog
cat
men
pin
bun
jog
bat
ten
fin
run
log

(Checklist sheet, one for each player)

Figure 28 Games using sounds

be an enjoyable and interesting experience shared by the teacher with her children and by parents with their children. Two other books in this series are concerned with different aspects of reading (Williams 1984 and Hedge 1984). Both books are full of ideas for the development of reading skills.

5.4 The Book Corner

A corner of the classroom can be set aside for a Book Corner. If no small bookshelves are available, the Book Corner can be made by pushing one or two flat-topped tables or desks into an angle of a corner of the classroom. A notice board can be arranged on the wall behind the tables or be placed on one of the tables resting against the wall. Books can be laid out flat on the tables, and one or two can be placed upright against the wall so that their covers can be seen more easily.

A Book Corner

Where it is not possible to keep the books on display in the Book Corner throughout the day, the children responsible (librarians) can pack them into cardboard cartons which can be stored in some safe corner.

The minimum number of books needed to start a Book Corner is the same as the number of children in the class. Gradually this number can be increased. In addition to books from official sources, other books can be obtained with money from school funds or class sales such as cake, jumble or 'bring and buy' sales, and by donations from parents (one book from each family every year). At the end of term one class's library can be exchanged with another class's library. If book buying has been co-ordinated, both classes should have a different or mostly different set of books for the new term.

CLASSIFICATION OF BOOKS

The main types of useful books can be classified into the following sections:

Graded and non-graded storybooks for Language 1 learners	S 1
Graded storybooks for ESL and EFL learners	S 2
Rhyme and song books	R
Information books	I
Dictionaries	D

Books in the Library can be numbered and listed, for example S 1/6, D/3.

Cassettes to accompany books can be bought or made by the teacher or native speaker visitors.

BORROWING CARDS

A borrowing card can be placed in a small envelope at the back of a book. The book numbers can be written on the envelope as well as inside the front cover and, if possible, on the spine of the book.

Books can be borrowed for a fixed period – one week is usual. During the holiday period more books can be taken out for a longer period (depending on the size of the library).

To borrow a book a child has to fill in his name and the date on the borrowing card, which he takes from the back of the book. At the same time he fills in a list of books borrowed that week by writing down his name and the name of the book borrowed (see Figure 29). This list forms for the teacher a weekly record of books

First Picture Dictionary	51/10	Date 2 Dec 1983	Librarians Olivier and Lilian
Name	Date	Borrower	Name of Book
Olivier Dang	Oct 7	Amina El Amrani	The very hungry caterpillar
		Saad Daoudi	Hide and Seek counting
		Youssef Tazi	Dinosaurs

Figure 29   Borrowing card and borrowing list

borrowed and their borrowers. Some teachers also ask children to keep a list of all the books they read over a term. This can be kept on a card or chart (see Figure 30).

Reading List	
Autumn Term 1983 Anna Lopez	
Title	Author
1. The Cat that Flew	Brian Taylor

Figure 30   Individual term reading list

LIBRARIANS

In the first weeks the teacher has to act as librarian to show children how to organise a library and what management language is needed. Once children understand, the teacher can take children in turn to work with her as assistant librarians. When enough children know how to be librarians and are able to communicate simply using prefabricated language, the teacher can appoint two children as librarians each month. The teacher can then become a borrower. The librarian's duties are:

1   to keep the library running efficiently
2   to check that borrowed books are returned
3   to make notices of new books
4   to help the teacher process new books.

All these duties should be carried out using English only.

NEW BOOKS

The teacher can introduce one new book each lesson or each week. In introducing a new book the teacher can tell, in simple English, enough details to make children want to read it. Thus she may tell part of a story leaving the children to read the end themselves. See Figure 31 for an example of a new book notice based on *How do I put it on?* by Watanabe (1979: 39).

Figure 31   A new book notice

Apart from giving children an opportunity to borrow books and to learn how a library works, a well-run library gives natural opportunities for communication and reading and writing practice.

5.5 Games

The choice of games which can be played in Part Two is greater than in Part One. The games can include some games played in

Part One but these games can now be played at a more difficult level to match children's increased listening, speaking and reading skills.

In selecting and organising games the following points should be considered:

1 Children are now more mature and less disturbed by losing a game, thus more games with individual competition can be included.

2 Children can now work in a group with a group leader, so can play team games with a team leader.

3 Children can now organise games by themselves without the teacher's supervision. Teachers may like to participate in games with the rest of the children, but should still be available to act as referee in cases of doubt.

4 Children can now read and write adequately for writing, crossword and other word puzzle games to be included.

5.6 Introducing cursive (joined) handwriting

Handwriting is so often neglected when teaching English to children whose own writing script is other than Roman script. It is up to teachers to lay the foundations so that children's handwriting is 'simultaneously legible, fast-flowing and individual and becomes effortless to produce' (The Bullock Report 1975: 11.50). These qualities are rarely picked up by chance. Children need guidance and opportunities for handwriting practice and these should be separate from activities where writing is primarily for communication.

Once children have reached a stage in physical and cognitive development when they can write print script quickly with correct stroke order (see Chapter 2), the cursive (joined) style of handwriting can be introduced. Most teachers find that children are not ready for this change before the age of eight or nine. Many children of this age find difficulty in making the complex letter shapes and in grasping the relation between the written and the printed forms. Many teachers of children who write Language 1 in another script, and have lessons only once or twice a week, have successfully delayed introducing cursive handwriting until children are ten years old.

SELECTING A HANDWRITING STYLE

The choice of handwriting style is generally decided by the school. In cases where the decision is left to the class teacher, teachers need to take care that children are not expected to change style each time they change class, as this is too confusing and demanding for children.

As transition to an adult writing style is difficult, many teachers find it easier for young children to learn a simplified joined handwriting (see Figure 32) which forms the foundation for the introduction later, when children are more mature, of an adult style of writing.

The teacher first introduces the letters of the alphabet in the same order as for print script (see Figure 11), with the following changes:

1   using more oval (egg) shapes
2   slanting about 7° to the right (ie not upright)
3   adding left and right joiners to letters.

The children can then make related patterns composed of letters as shown in Steps One and Two. These patterns help children to get the flow of a cursive handwriting.

After Step Three in the structured programme children can begin to write words.

Capital (upper case) letters are the same as in print script. Capitals do not join on to small (lower case) letters. In the initial stages small letters immediately after a capital begin with a joiner although they are not joined. As skill and speed increase these

Figure 32 Structured programme for simplified joined handwriting

Steps	Letters	Related patterns	Words for writing practice	Notes
Step one	i l	ililililil		*Left join – half way up letter* *Right join – at bottom of letter*
Step two	v w	rrrrrrr wwwww		*Right and left joins – horizontal*
Step three	n m h	nnnnnnn in him nnhnnnh win		*Left join – half way up letter* *Right join – at bottom of letter*
Step four	r p b	rrrrrn lip pin phnphn bin		*Left join – half way up letter* *Right join for r – horizontal (none for p and b)*
Step five	o a e	aeaeaeae he men amama pen hop man arm hen ear		*Left and right join for o – horizontal* *Left join for a and e – half way up letter, right join – at bottom of letter*

Steps	Letters	Related patterns	Words for writing practice	Notes
Step six	c d g q	cdhcdh cogcog	come leg dog bag car egg bird girl	*Left join* – half way up letter as in a *Right join* for c and d at bottom of letter (none for g and q)
Step seven	u s z	umumu duldul	sun his bus zoo she house school good	*Left join* – half way up for u and s (none for z) *Right join* at bottom of letter for u (none for s and z)
Step eight	f j t	fufufuf	it cat tree fat flag hat train flow	*Left join* – half way up letter *Right join* – horizontal for f, at the bottom of letter for t (none for j)
Step nine	x y k	dyidyi ox ox	toy book boy kid eye nose	*Left join* – none for x except horizontal with o, half way up letter for y and k *Right join* – at bottom of letter for k, no right join for x and y

left-hand joiners can be dropped. In the same way left-hand joiners at the beginning of a word can be dropped.

Initial stages | **Cursive writing**

Ann
dog

Ann
dog

HANDWRITING PRACTICE
Children who write for most of the day in another script in another direction (for example in Arabic from right to left or in Japanese from top to bottom of the page) need regular handwriting practice.

Opportunities can be given either in the lesson or for homework, to copy:

1 school messages, notices, invitations
2 words already done, to make fair copies to be pasted into class or school books
3 greeting, birthday cards
4 anthologies of poems and prose.

Materials
Experience of writing both on lined and unlined, white and coloured paper as well as paper of different shapes is important. Different writing implements can be used. However, to get an even flow using ink it is best to use a medium nib. Children who write Language 1 in a different script should be encouraged to have a special pen for writing English. Left-handed children may need a left-handed pen.

HANDWRITING MODELS
Every possible opportunity should be taken to write notices, labels, lists, titles under paintings or drawings, etc, so that

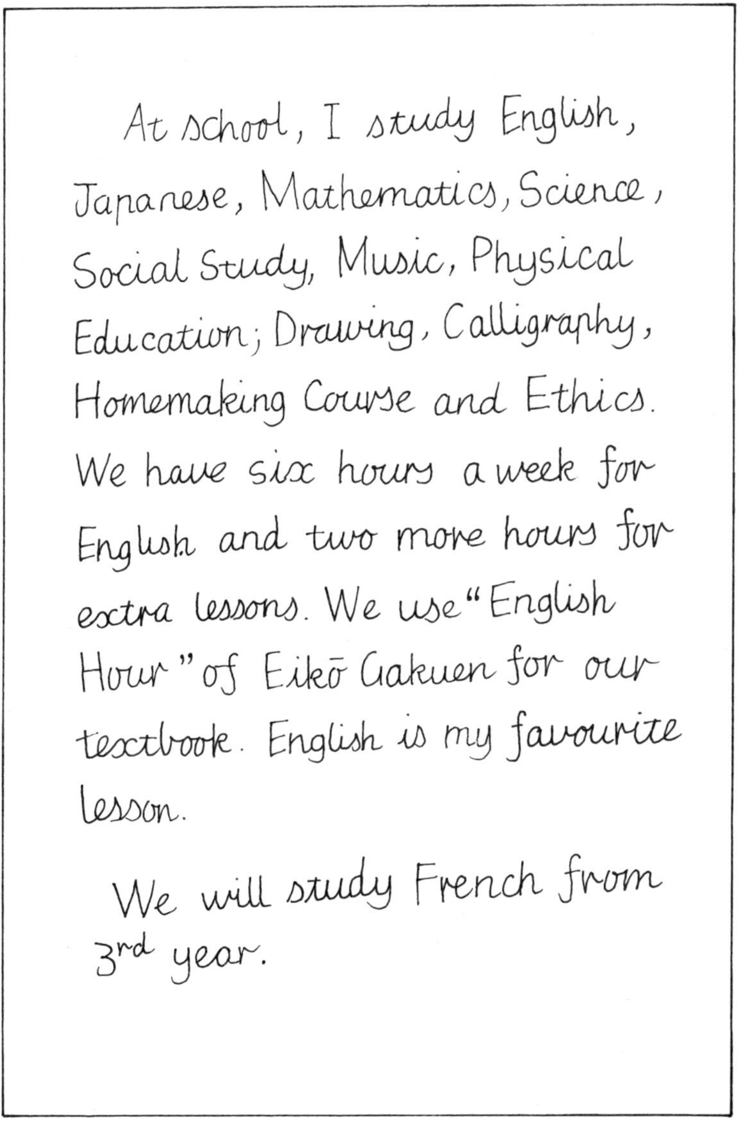

At school, I study English, Japanese, Mathematics, Science, Social Study, Music, Physical Education; Drawing, Calligraphy, Homemaking Course and Ethics. We have six hours a week for English and two more hours for extra lessons. We use "English Hour" of Eikō Gakuen for our textbook. English is my favourite lesson.

We will study French from 3rd year.

Figure 33 Joined handwriting (see Figure 10 for earlier writing by the same child)

children are continually exposed to good examples of handwriting. Of course these notices need to be changed frequently otherwise children get used to them and no longer bother to read them.

Writing on the blackboard should also be of a high standard; any slight difference in a letter shape at this stage tends to get copied as children still have not sufficient experience to predict what a badly shaped letter is intended to represent. (Some teachers find that they have to practise handwriting themselves at home to get their blackboard writing to an acceptable standard.)

It is a good idea to keep examples of good handwriting done by children, or messages received from other children or staff, in a class book in the Book Corner. Children seem to like looking through this type of book and making comments; they also seem to learn from other people's work.

5.7 A final word

From time to time teachers might ask themselves if their lessons are:

		✓	×
1	fun		
2	interesting and lively		
3	motivating		
4	well-planned		
5	fitting into a scheme of work		
6	giving consolidation		
7	using only English		

Teachers could also check that their children are:

	✓	✗
1 secure		
2 satisfied		
3 successful		
4 speaking more English each lesson		
5 enjoying story and rhyme books in English		

References

Abbs B and Worrall A, *Jigsaw Activity Book 1*, (London: Mary Glasgow, 1979).

Bowen B Morgan, *Look Here! Visual Aids in Language Teaching*, (London: Macmillan, 1982).

The Bullock Report, *A Language for Life*, (London: HMSO, 1975).

Dunn O, *Mr Bear's Book of Rhymes*, (London: Macmillan, 1979a).

Dunn O, *Read and Write with Black and White (Workbook 1)*, (London: Macmillan, 1979b).

Dunn O, *Read and Write with Black and White (Workbook 2)*, (London: Macmillan, 1979c).

Dunn O, *Red Hen's Cake (Ranger* Story Workbooks), (London: Macmillan, 1979d).

Dunn O, *Beginning English with young children*, (London: Macmillan, 1983).

Gollasch F V (ed), *Language and Literacy: the selected writings of Kenneth Goodman*, (London: Routledge and Kegan Paul, 1982).

Hedge P, *Using Graded Readers*, (London: Macmillan, 1984).

Holden S, *Teaching children*, (London: Modern English Publications, 1980).

Mackay D, Thompson B and Schaub P, *Breakthrough to Literacy*, (London: Longman, 1970).

Morris J M et al, *Language in Action* (The Language Project), (London: Macmillan Education, 1974).

Murray W, *Key Words Reading Scheme*, (Loughborough: Ladybird Books, 1969).

Nichols R, *Helping your Child to Read*, (London: Centre for Teaching of Reading, Reading University, n.d.).

Rixon S, *My English Workbook 1*, (London: Macmillan, 1980).

Rixon S, *How to use games in language teaching*, (London: Macmillan, 1981).

Tench P, *Pronunciation skills*, (London: Macmillan, 1981).

Watanabe S, *How do I put it on?* (London: The Bodley Head, 1979).

Williams E, *Reading in the language classroom*, (London: Macmillan, 1984).

Useful books

Go, G Broughton (London: Longman).

Key Words Reading Scheme, W Murray (Loughborough: Ladybird Books).

Language in Action (The Language Project), Project Director: Dr Joyce M Morris (London: Macmillan).

Rangers, General editor: Carol Christian (London: Macmillan).

Ranger Story Workbooks, (London: Macmillan).